Impossibly Opossum
Coloring Book, Facts, and Games

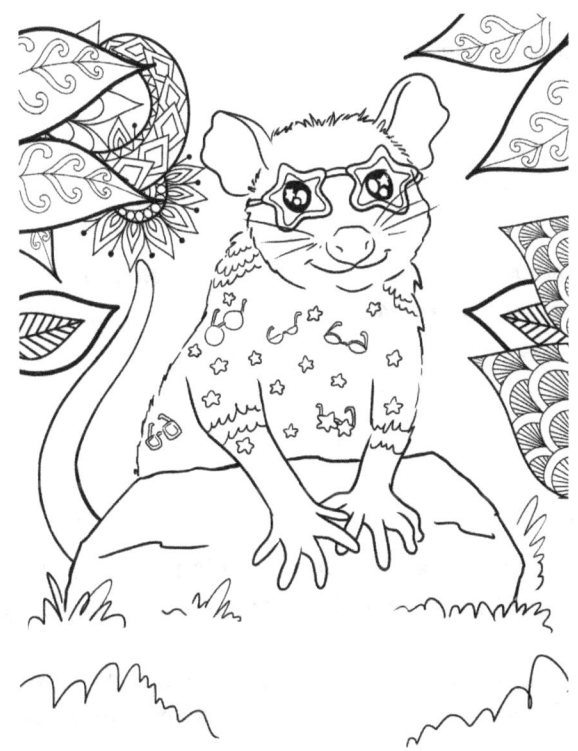

Dr. Jonathan Terry

Dr. Jonathan Terry
Walnut, CA
United States
2020

Impossibly Opossum: Coloring Book, Facts, and Games

Copyright © 2020 by Dr. Jonathan Terry

All rights reserved. No part of this book may be reproduced or transmitted in
any form or by any means without written permission.

ISBN: 9798668229253

Names, characters, events, and incidents are the products of the editor's imagination;
any resemblance to actual images, persons, animals, or actual events is purely coincidental.

Proceeds from the sales of this coloring book may be used to fund mental health initiatives
at the discretion of the editor. For more information, please visit www.mycapybara.com.

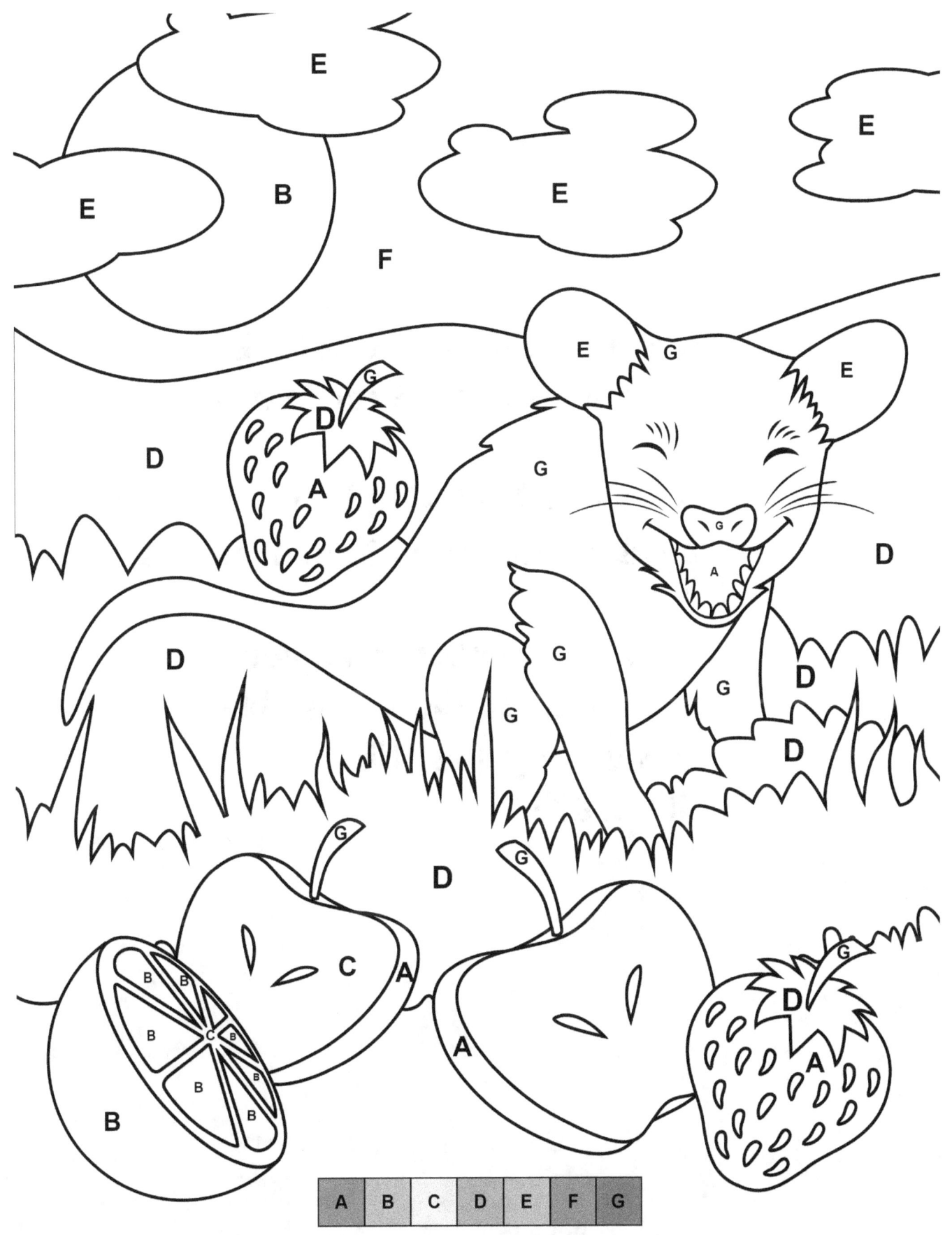

Our first coloring book took us to the cutest of capybaras.

Our second coloring book bamboo-zled us with pandas.

For book number three, we wanted to do the impossible - so we bring you THE OPOSSUM!

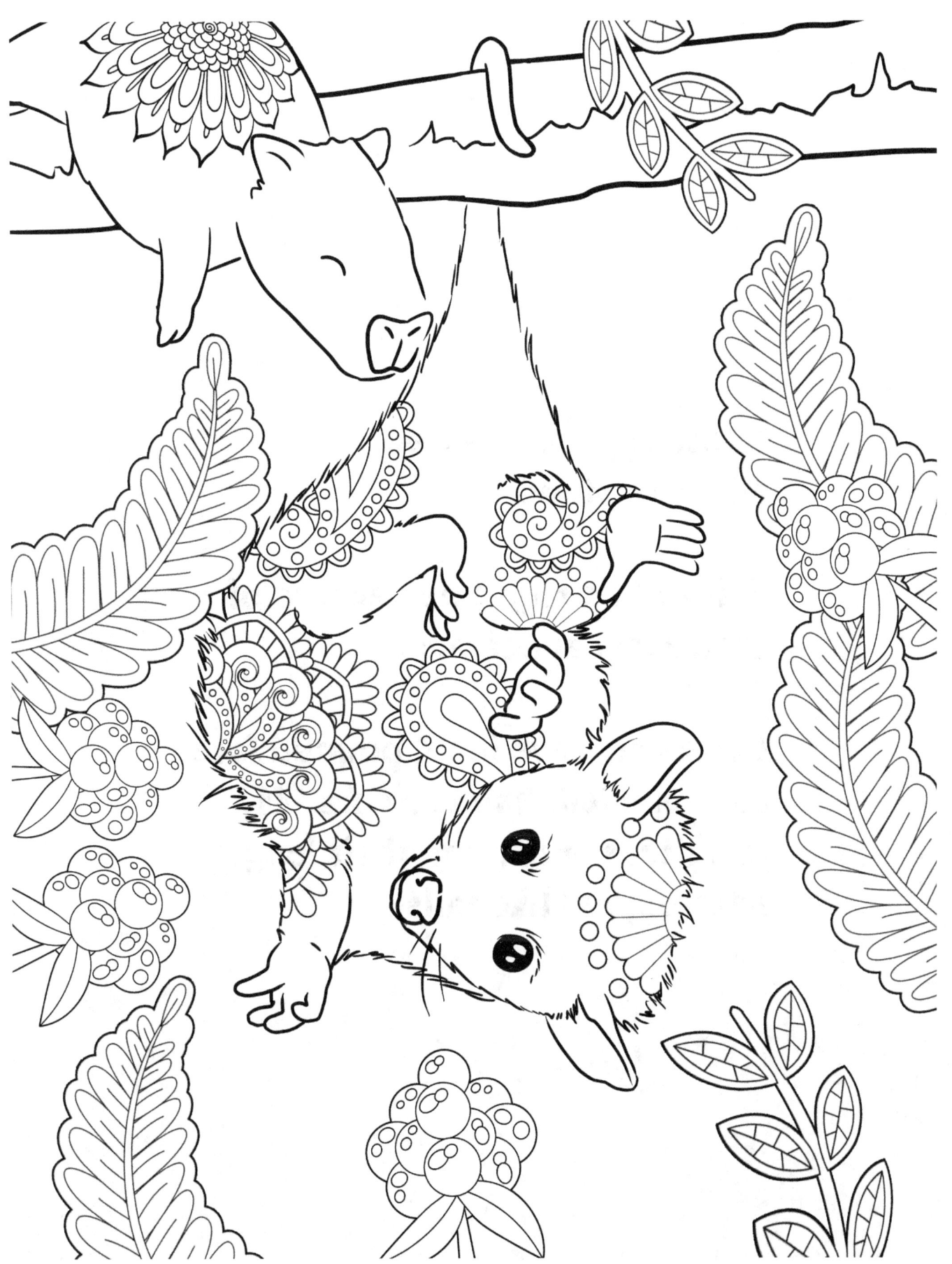

Opossums are so often misunderstood.

Part of this might be because of their scary appearance.

Opossums have long, pointed faces and rounded, hairless ears. My favorite, though, are their long, hairless, rat-like tails.

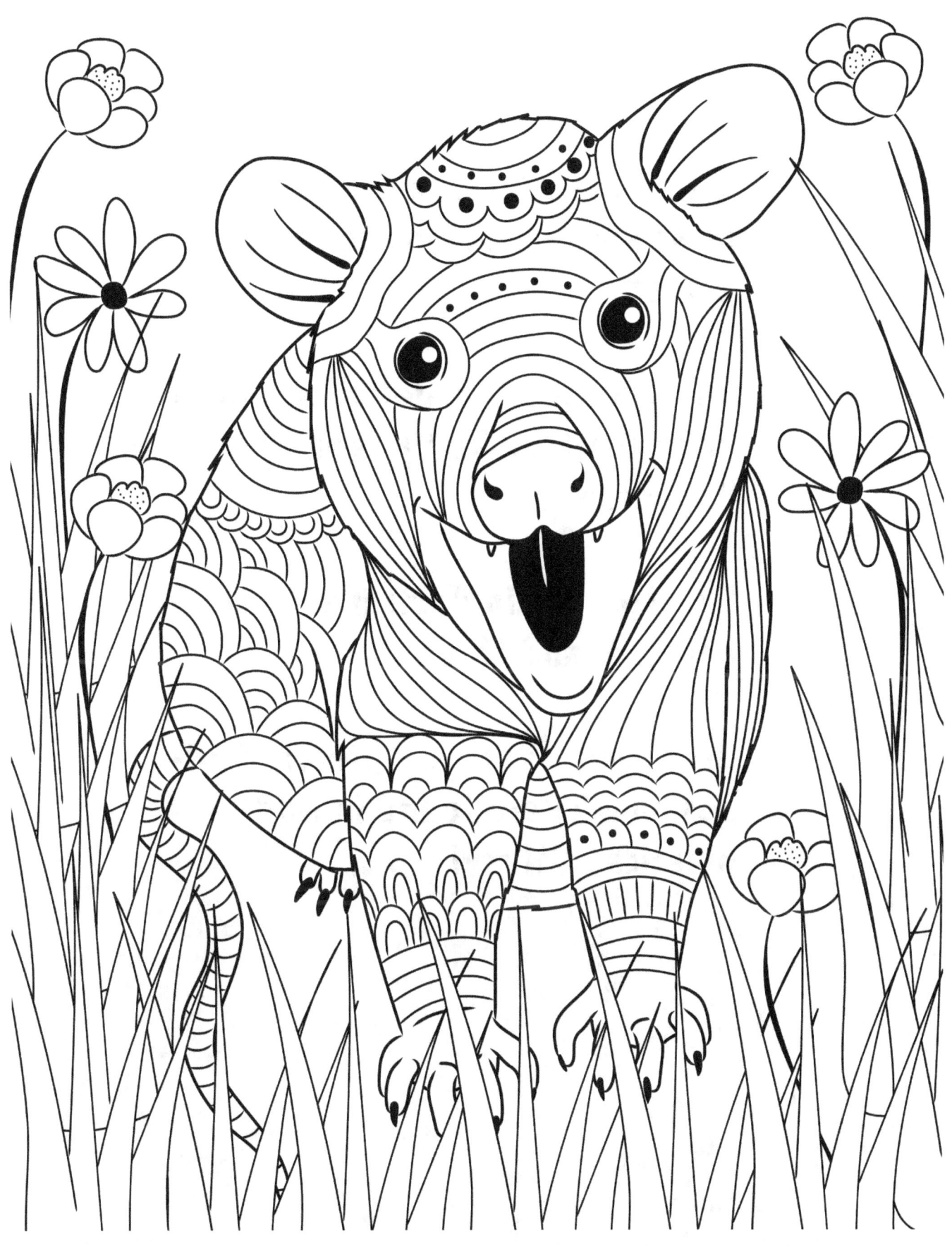

Let's take a look at the map and make sure we're on the same planet.

An "opossum" is definitely not a "possum," and a "possum" isn't an "opossum"!

Possums are in Australia, New Zealand, and China.

Opossums (or if you prefer, "OH-possums") are found in North America. OH my!

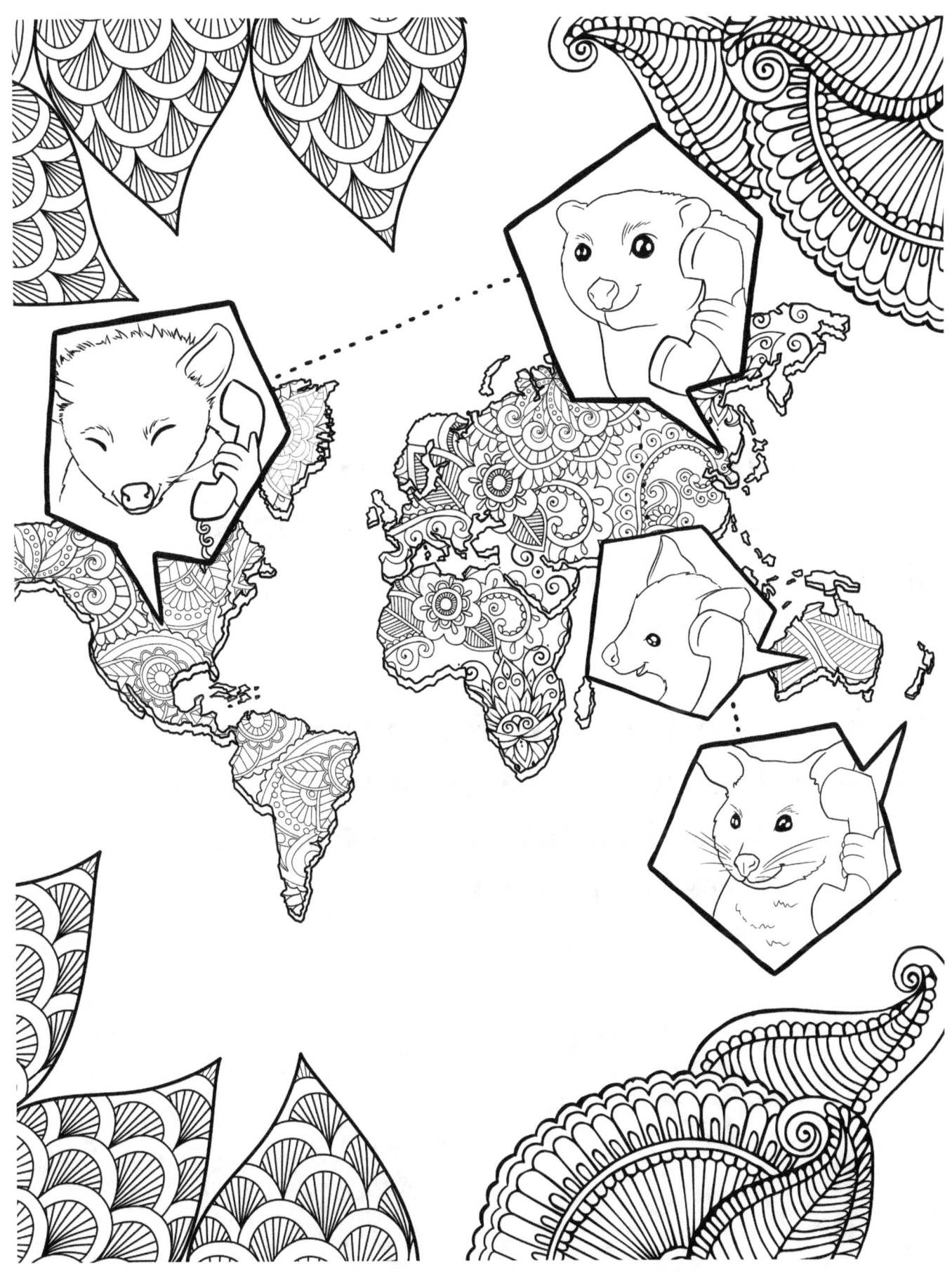

Possums (without the "o") are more closely related to Australian marsupials. This means every day for them is a g'day!

They look a bit like a squirrel and chinchilla combined to form a squi-chilla. Now that would be an awesome possum!

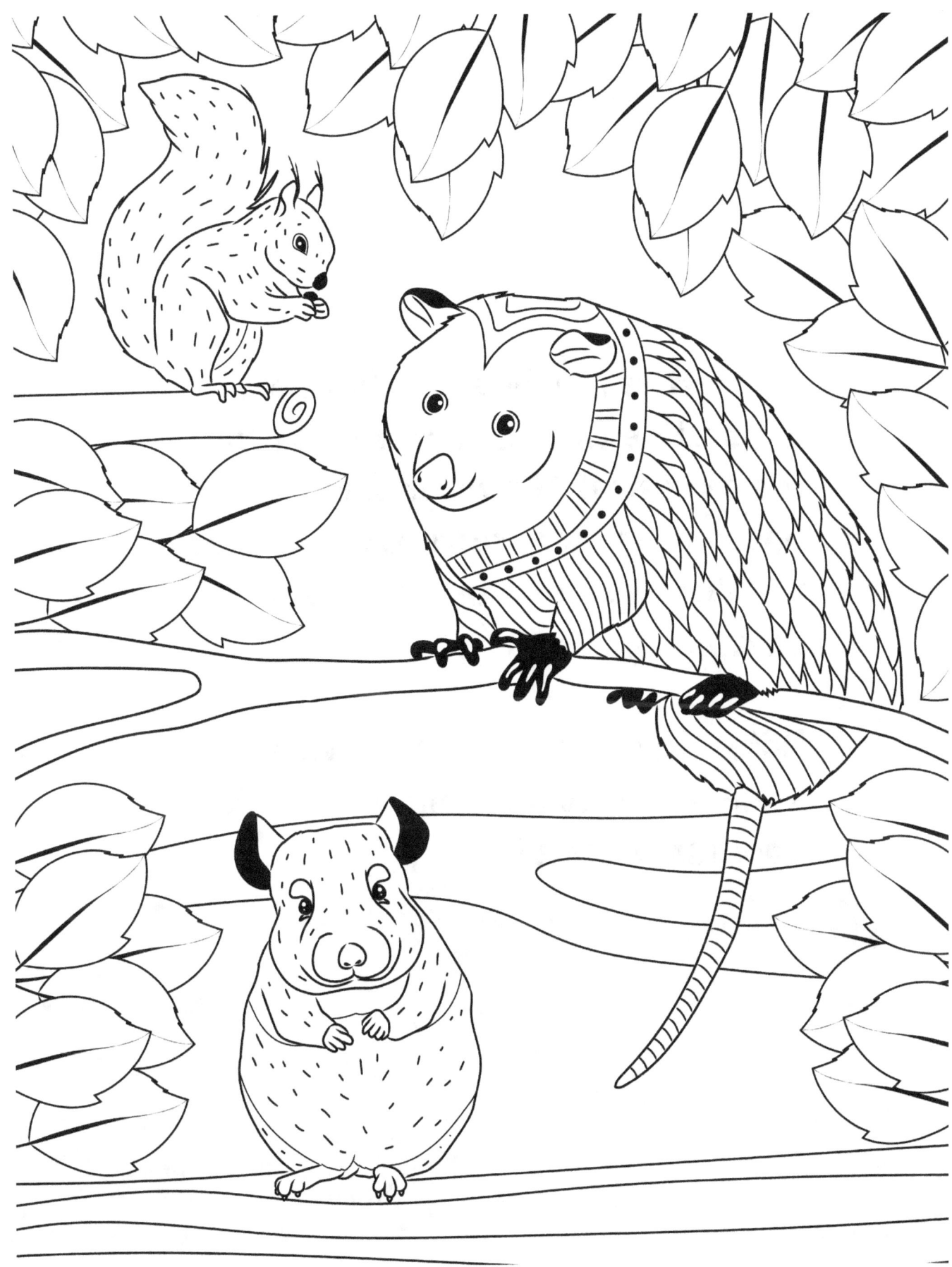

The rest of this book is about the impossible tick magnet we all love: the opossum! The North American opossum is more correctly known as the Virginia opossum (*Didelphis virginiana*).

Note: ticks here are *not* drawn to scale, but they are a big part of the opossum's story!

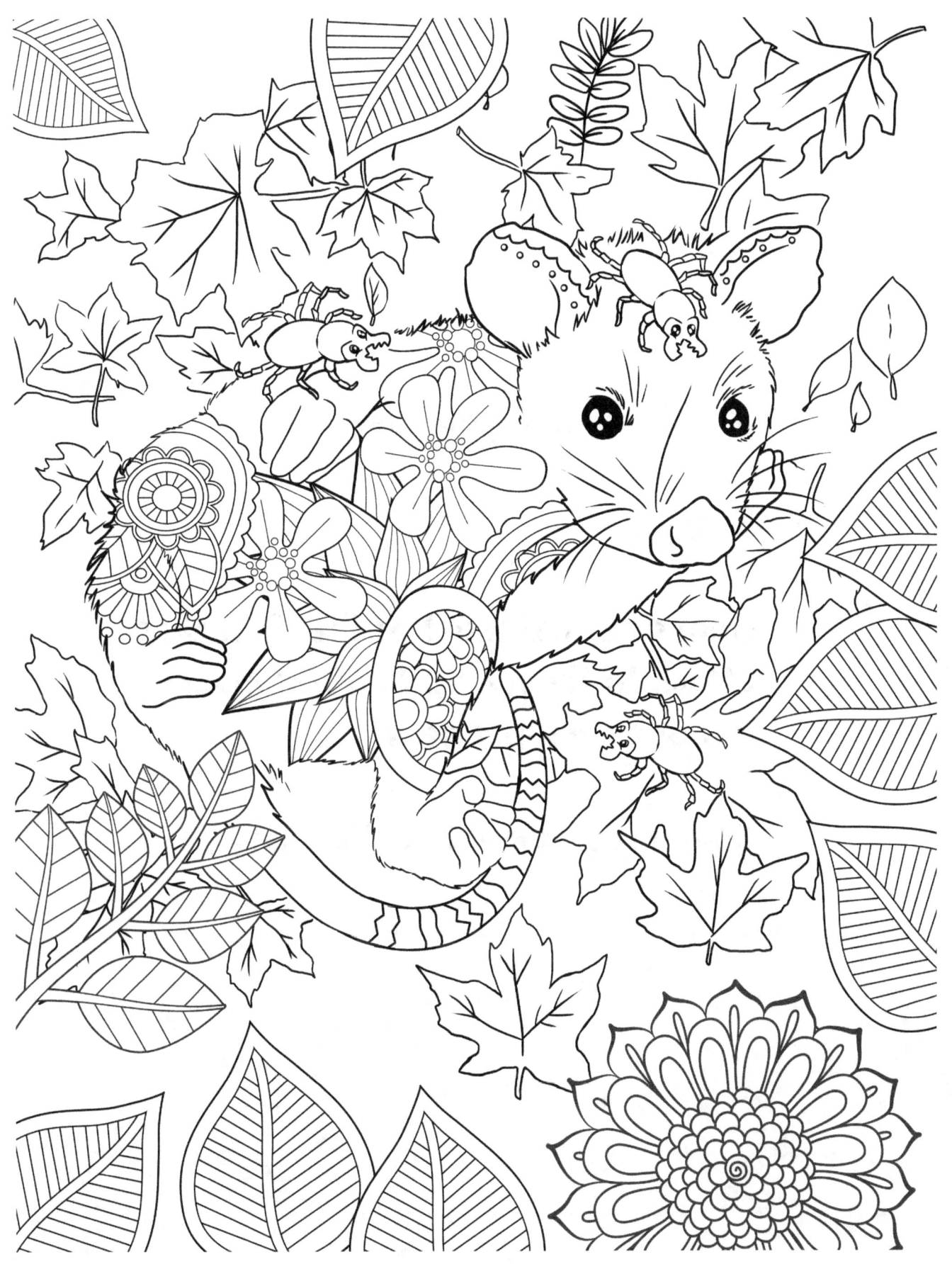

A tick magnet, you say?

Why yes!

Opossums eat most of the ticks that attach to them - up to 5000 insects per opossum per year!

How impossumably delicious!

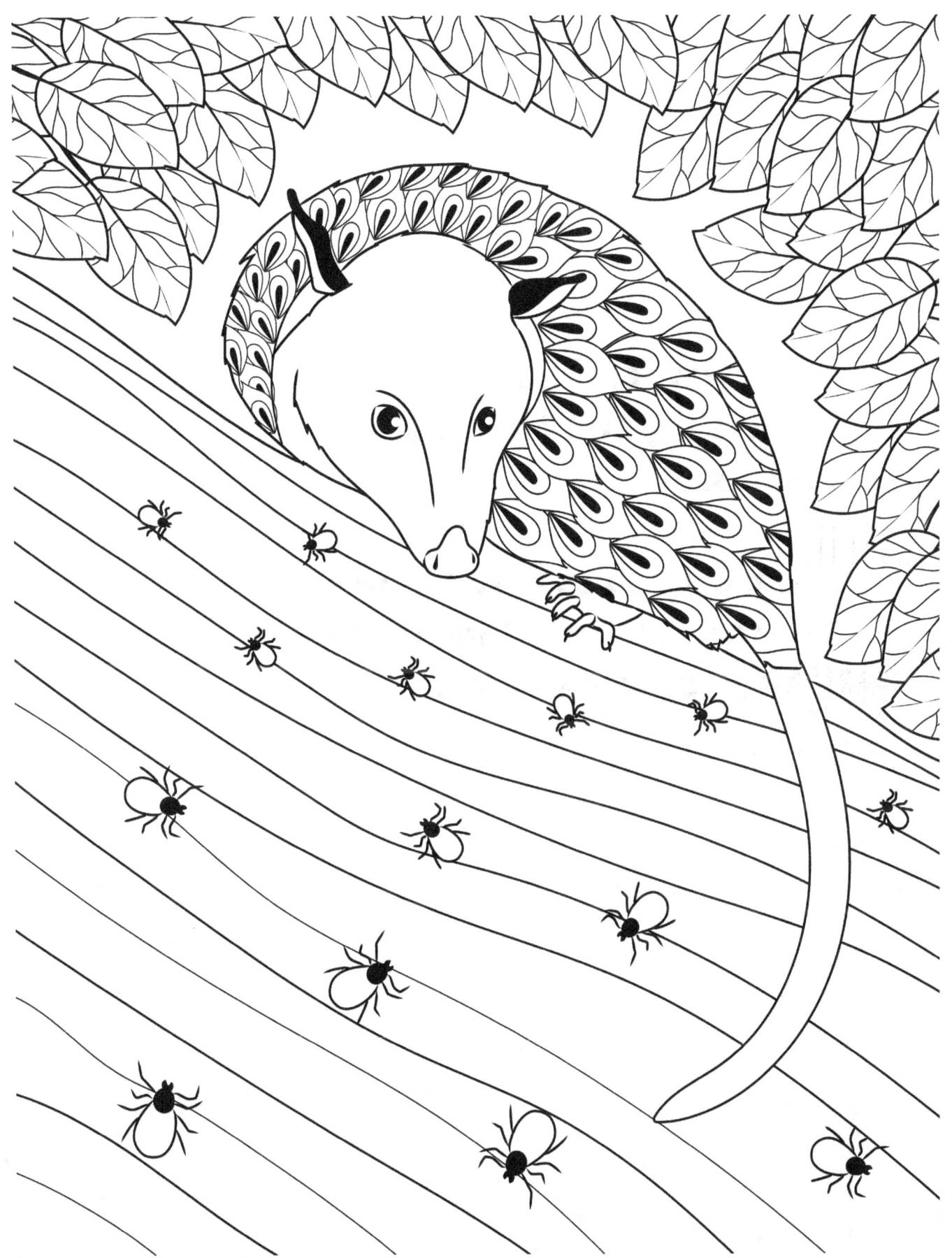

With way less ticks than a clock, others say that opossums spread rabies.

Actually, rabies is very rare in opossums! Part of the reason for this is their low body temperature.

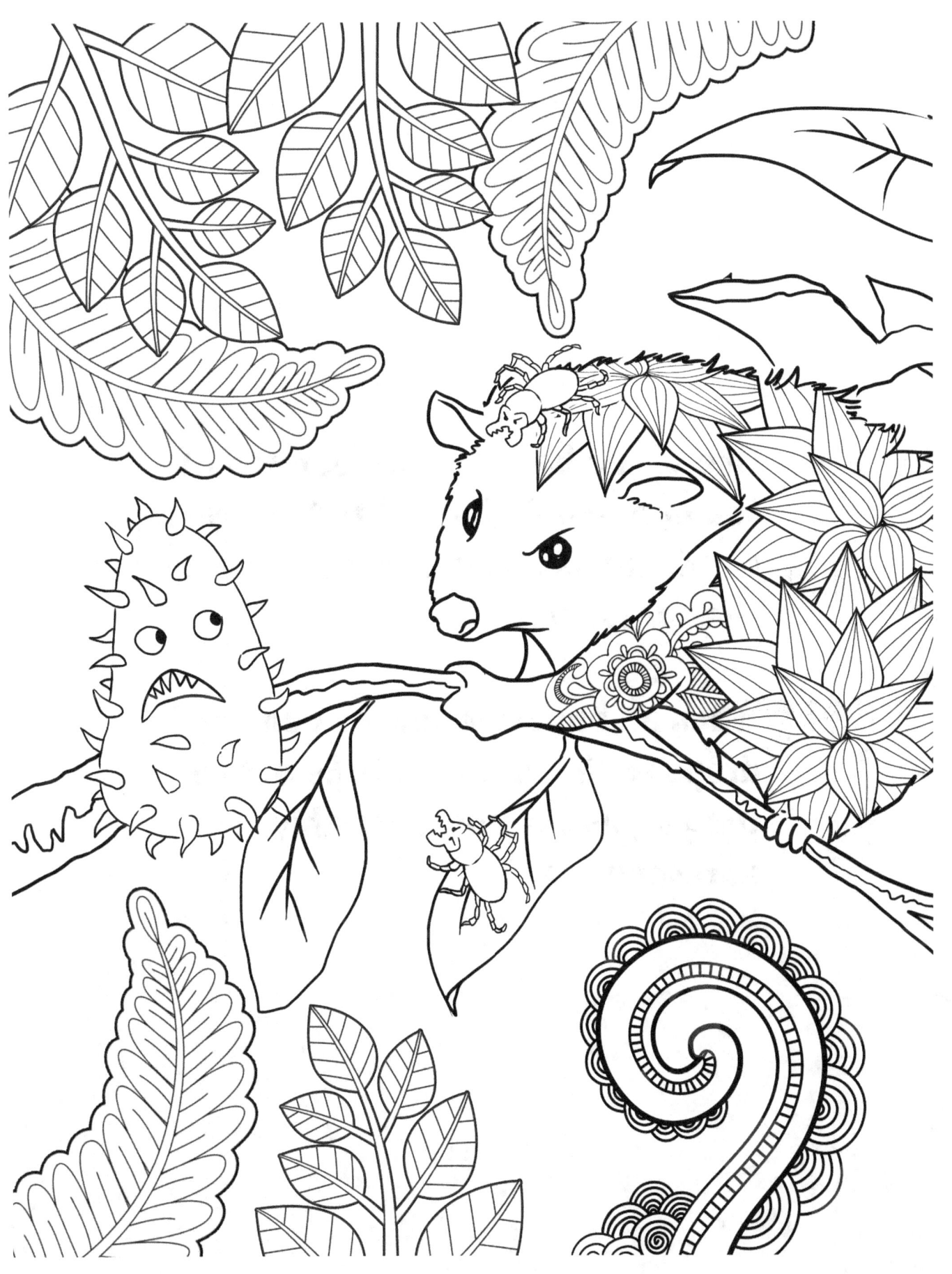

One of the best-known features of the opossum is its ability to play dead…or as some might say, to *play possum*!

When an opossum senses danger, it drops to the ground, sticks out its tongue, and is opossum-ably unresponsive.

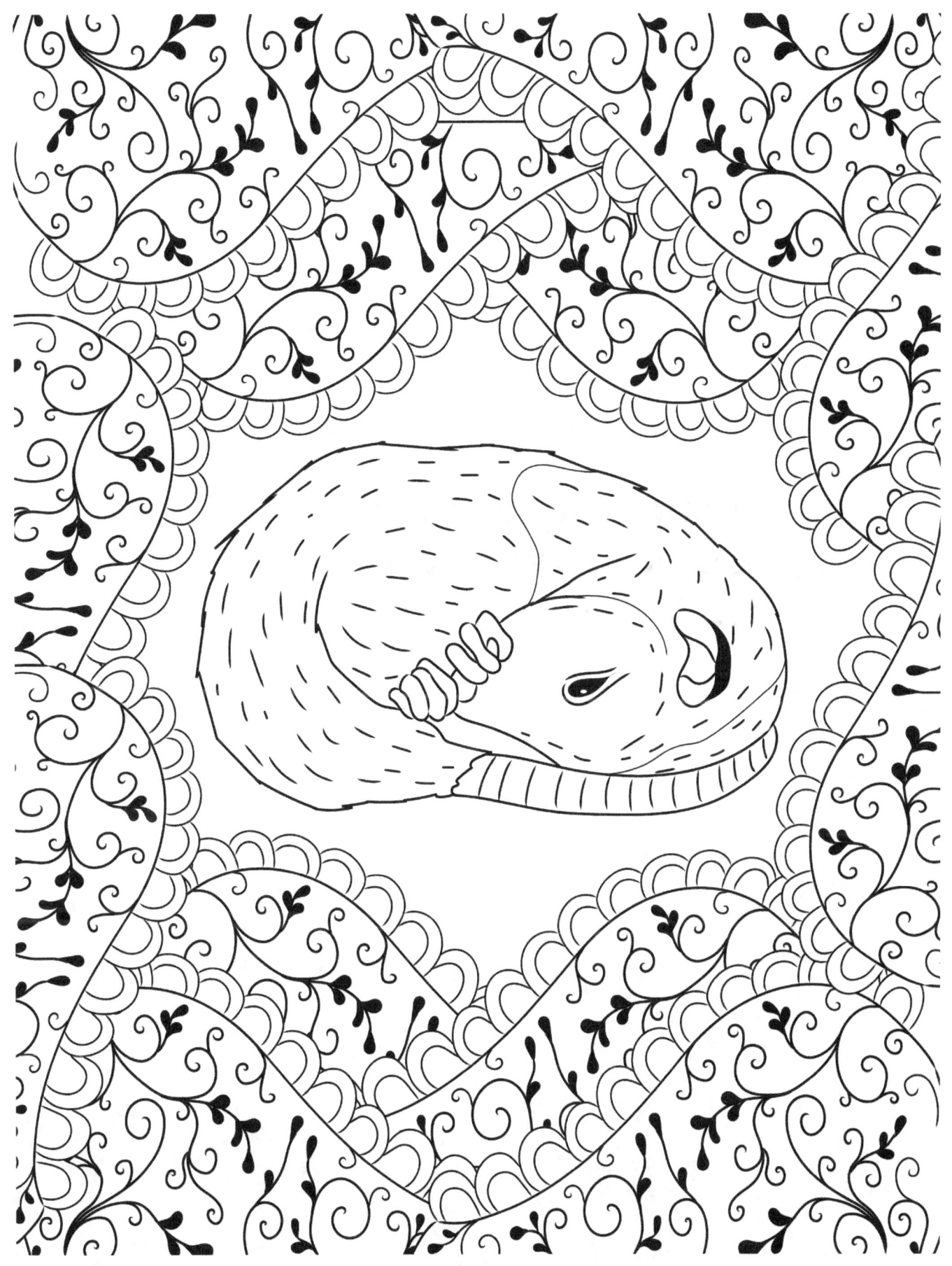

During these periods, the opossum's heart rate drops and breathing slows.

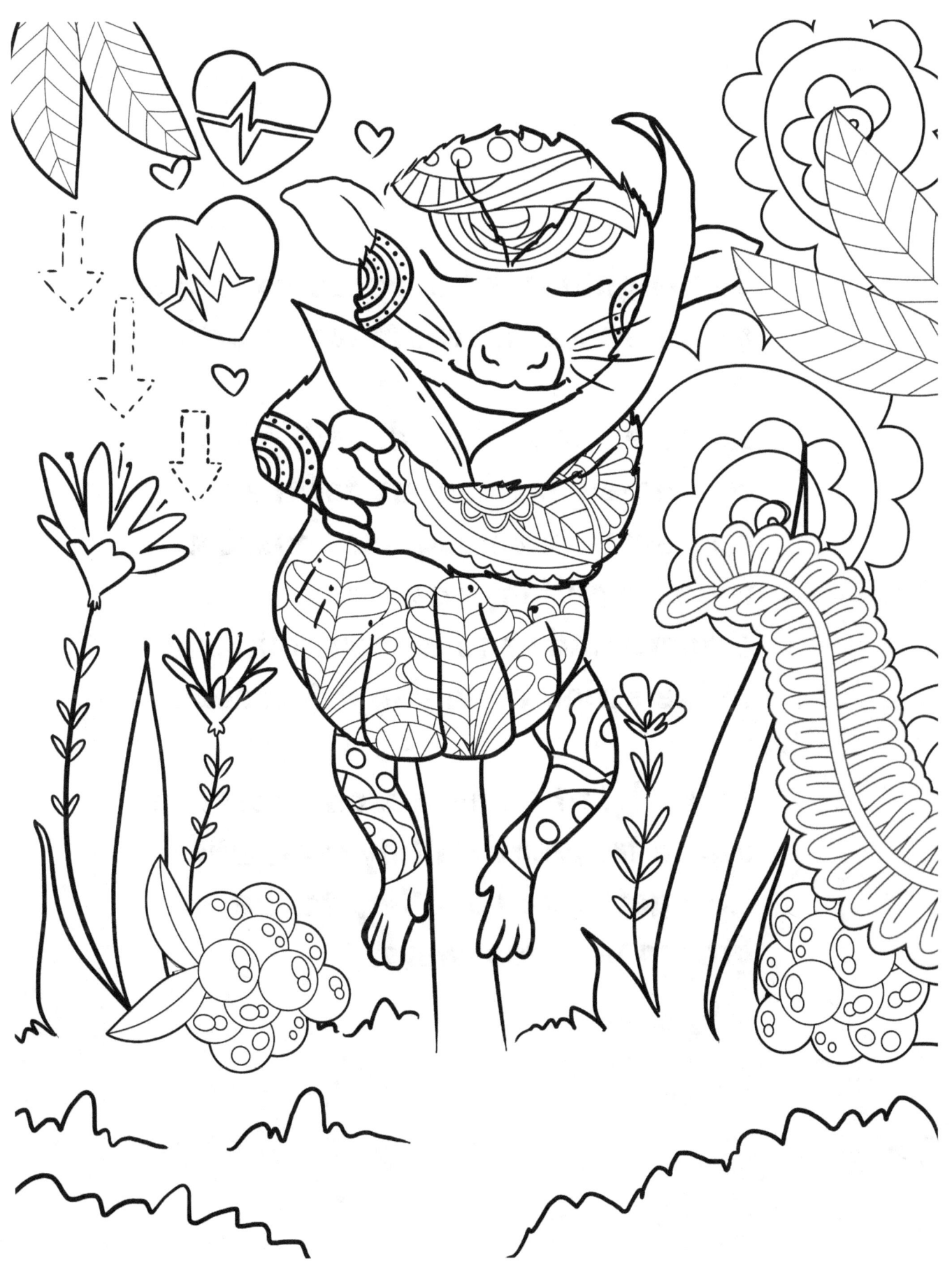

You might think the opossum should get an Academy Award for its acting.

However, the "drop dead" skill is completely involuntary for the opossum – meaning our opossum friend can "play possum" automatically and without thinking of the action or willing it to happen.

This might be one reason opossums are so frequently hit by cars, when they get scared and flop to the ground near roadways.

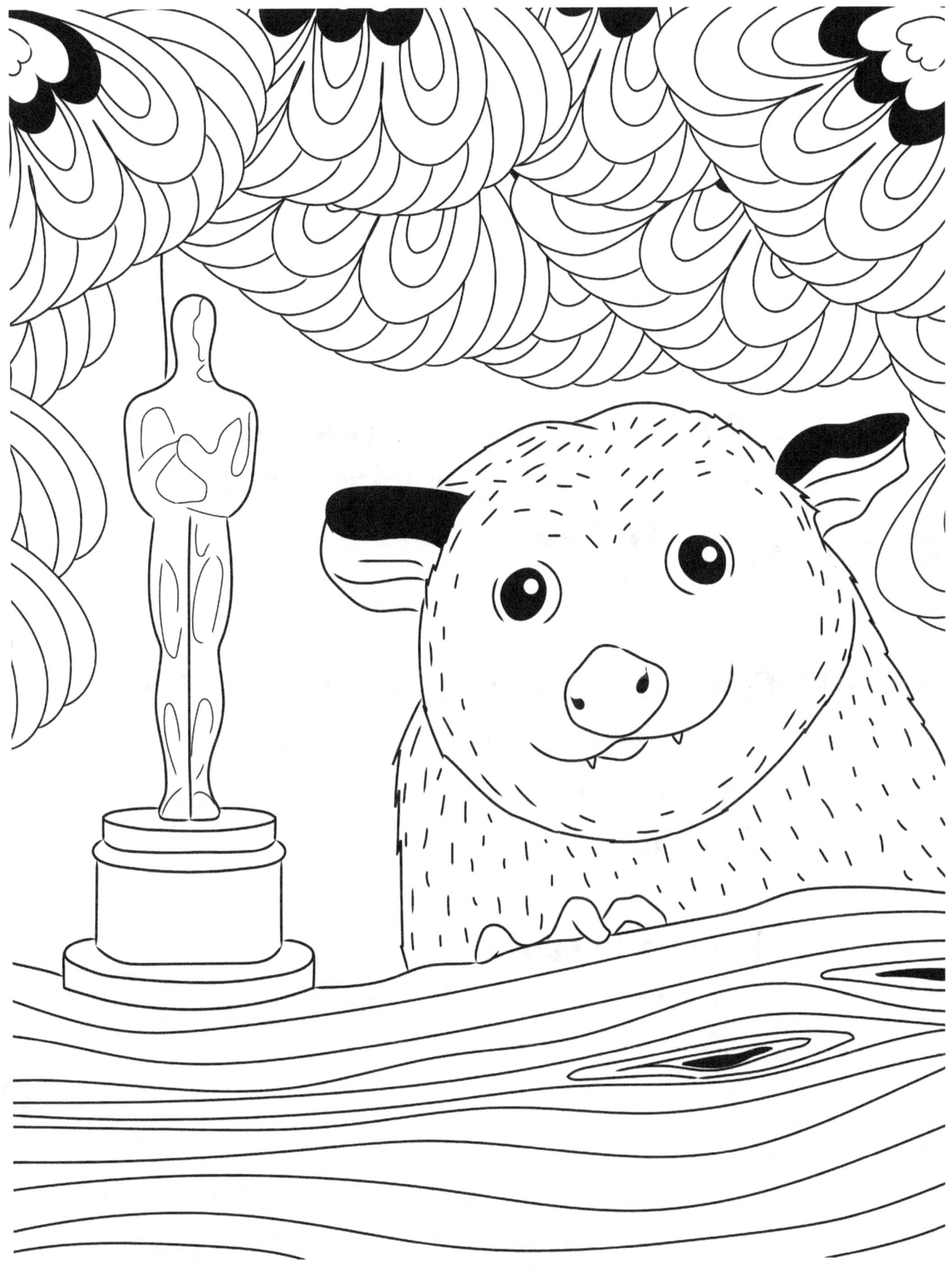

What's that smell?! If you said "a dead opossum" you might be right. You might also be temporarily mistaken.

You see, even when opossums "play dead" they make a super stinky "death-like" odor from glands near their butt.

How *very* skunky!

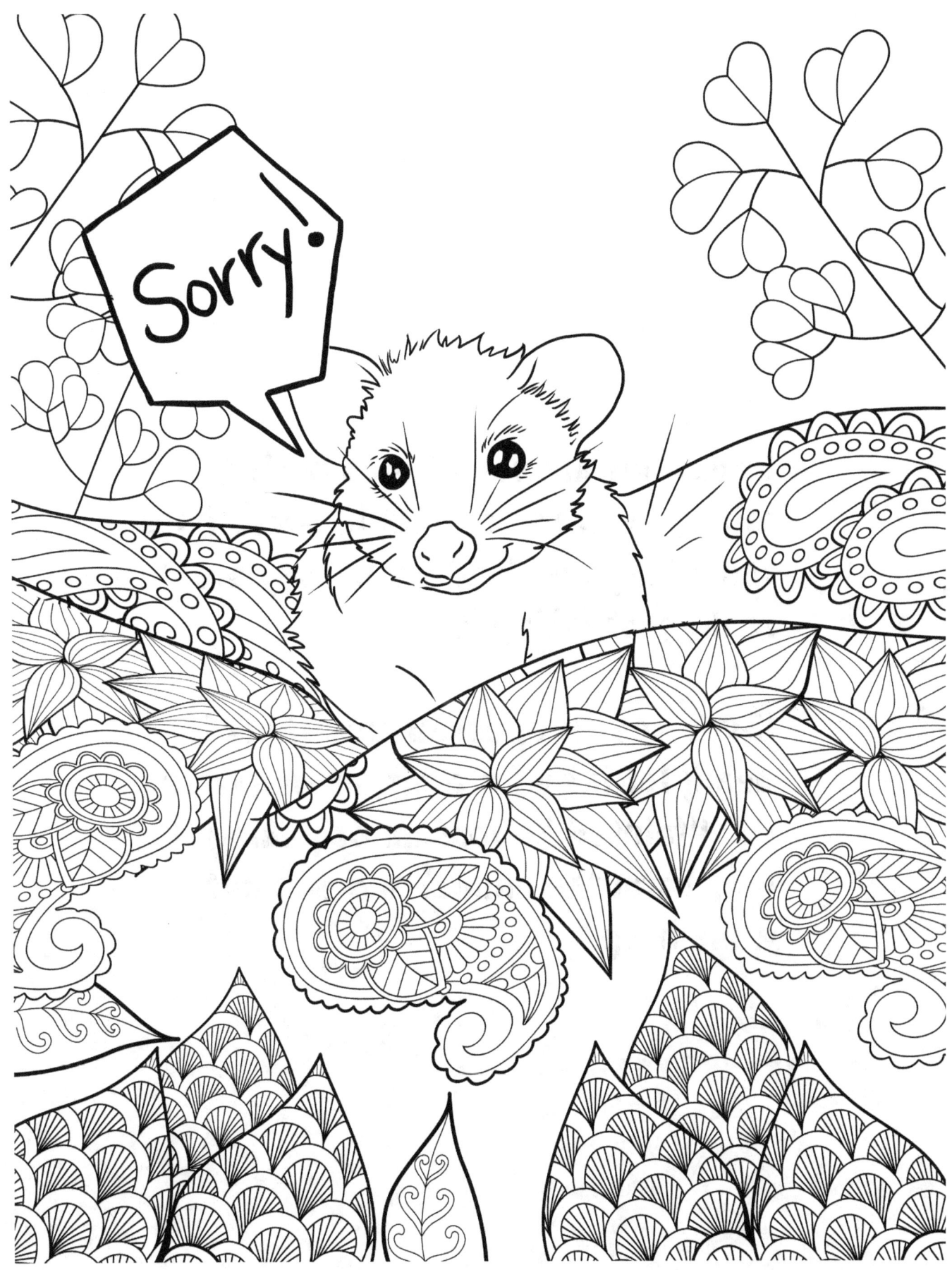

Opossums are sometimes buried alive or discarded; people sometimes think they are dead when they are really just faking it.

If you see an opossum you think is dead, let it be for a bit, as disturbing the "fainted" opossum or poking it may harm the animal and will not wake it up.

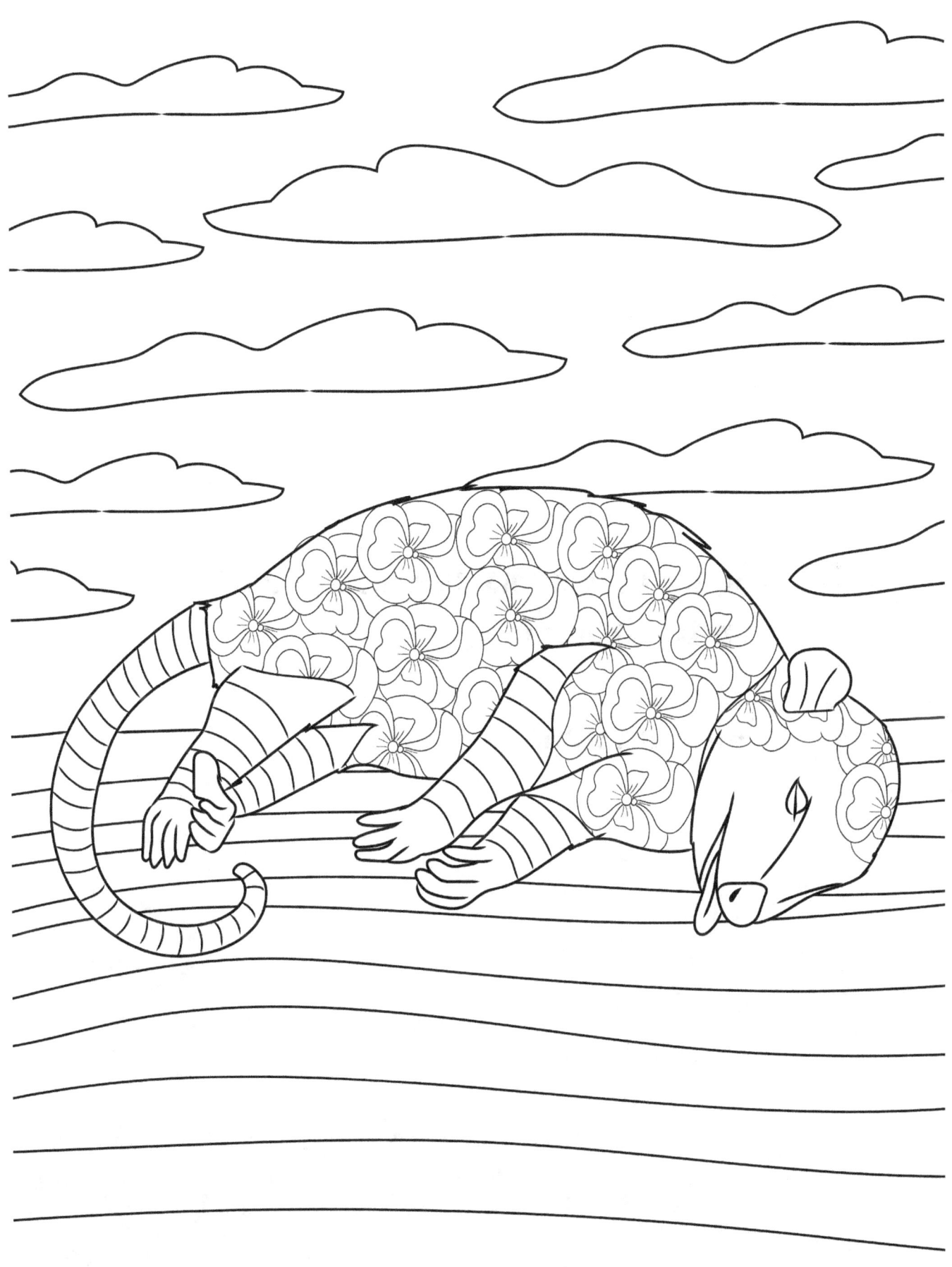

Some opossums can feign death for up to six hours.

What a talent!

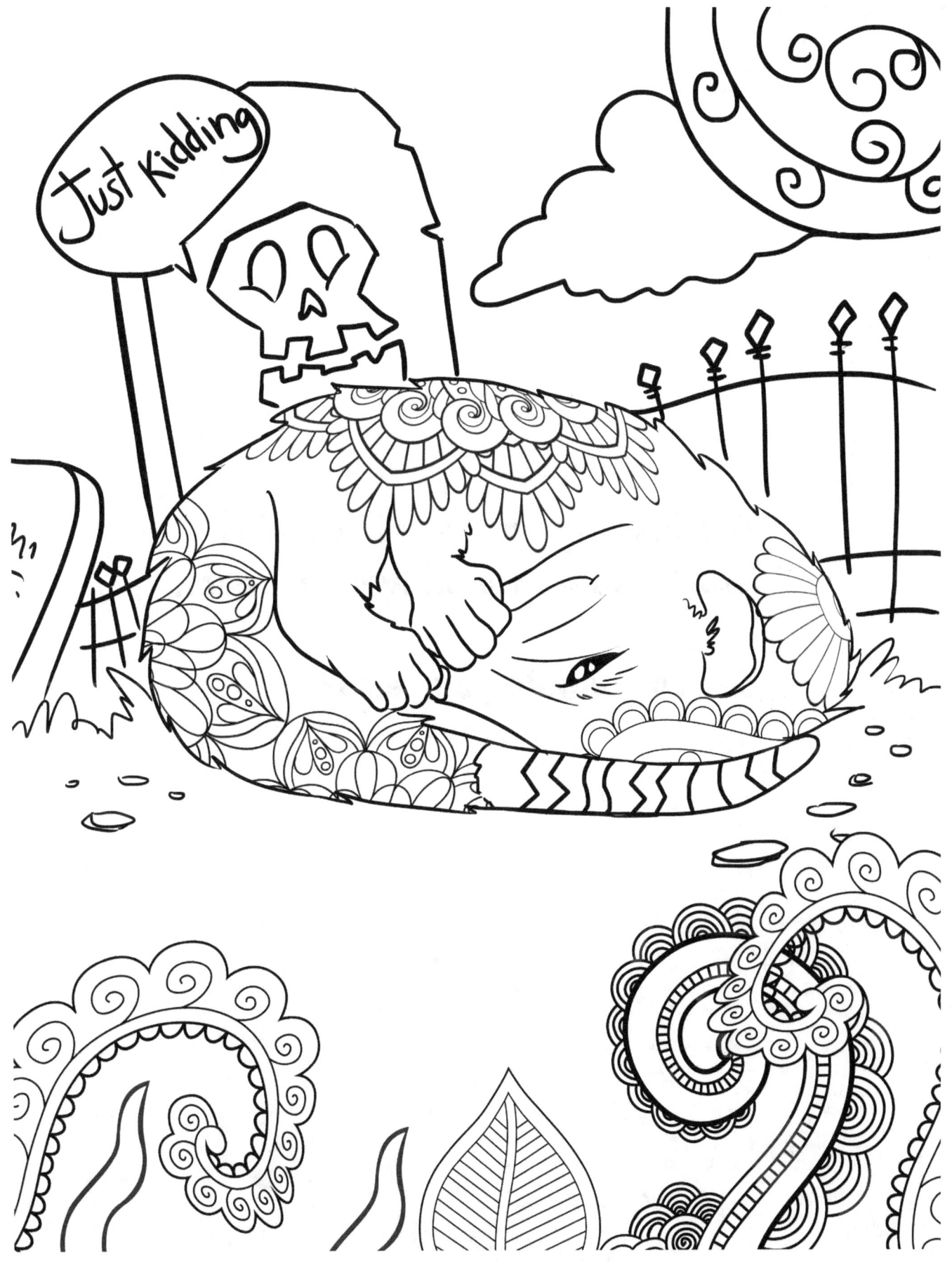

The first sign of "waking up" is usually some wiggling of the ears.

Can you wiggle your ears?

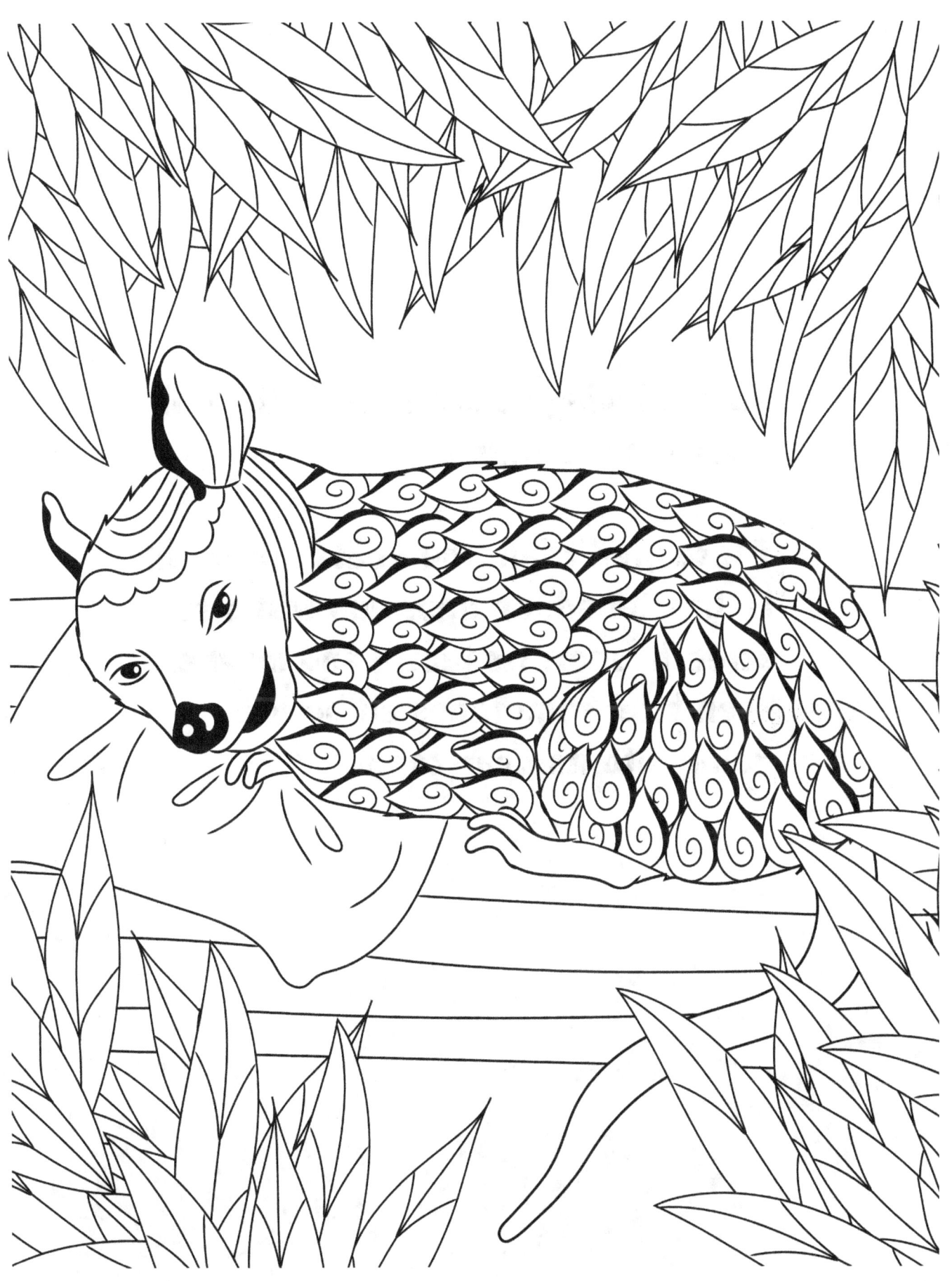

Now "playing possum" isn't the only opossum's defense.

These aren't fainting goats, after all! If threatened, an opossum will hiss, screech, show its teeth, and maybe even bite, sometimes all before going into its near-coma.

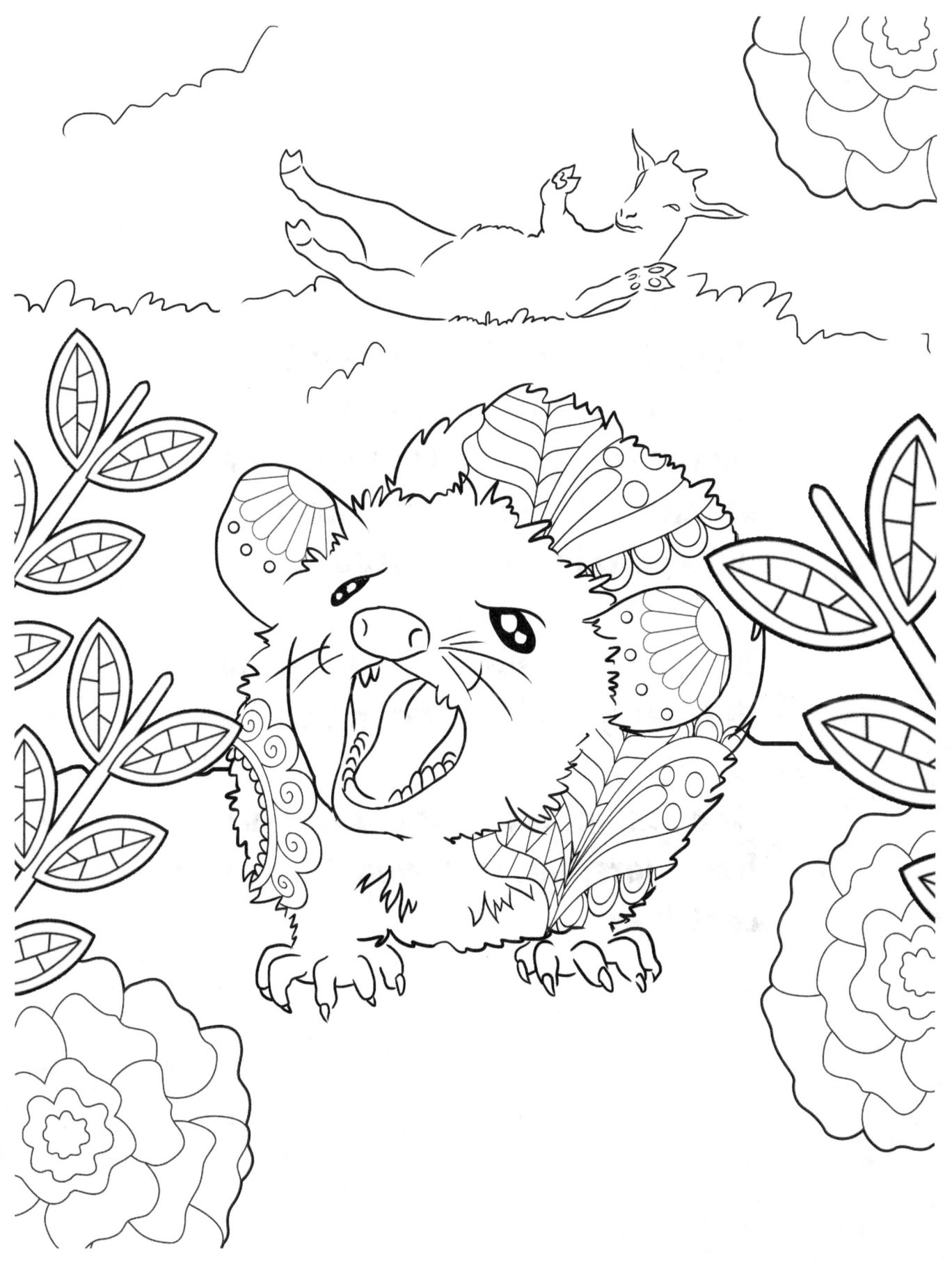

If you think you're starting to get this animal "in the pouch," we should remind you that opossums are the only marsupial found in the United States and Canada.

What is a marsupial? This means they carry their young in pouches.

[It does not mean opossums are from Mars, but that would be really cool.]

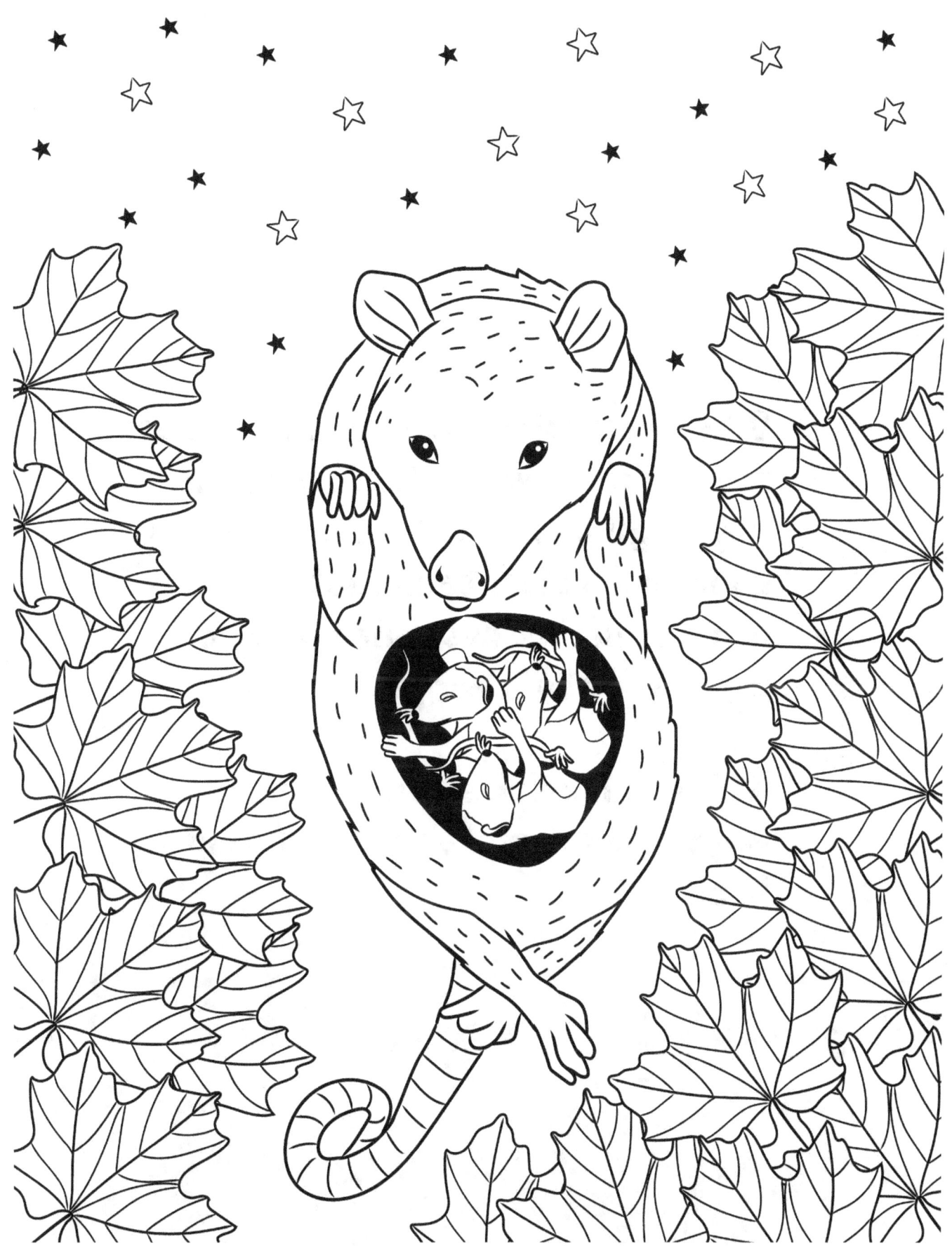

Other marsupials include 330 species ranging from wombats, Tasmanian devils, gliders, kangaroos, wallabies, quokkas, koalas, bandicoots, and…even that Australian possum we talked about earlier.

Which marsupial is your favorite? Maybe we can make you a coloring book!

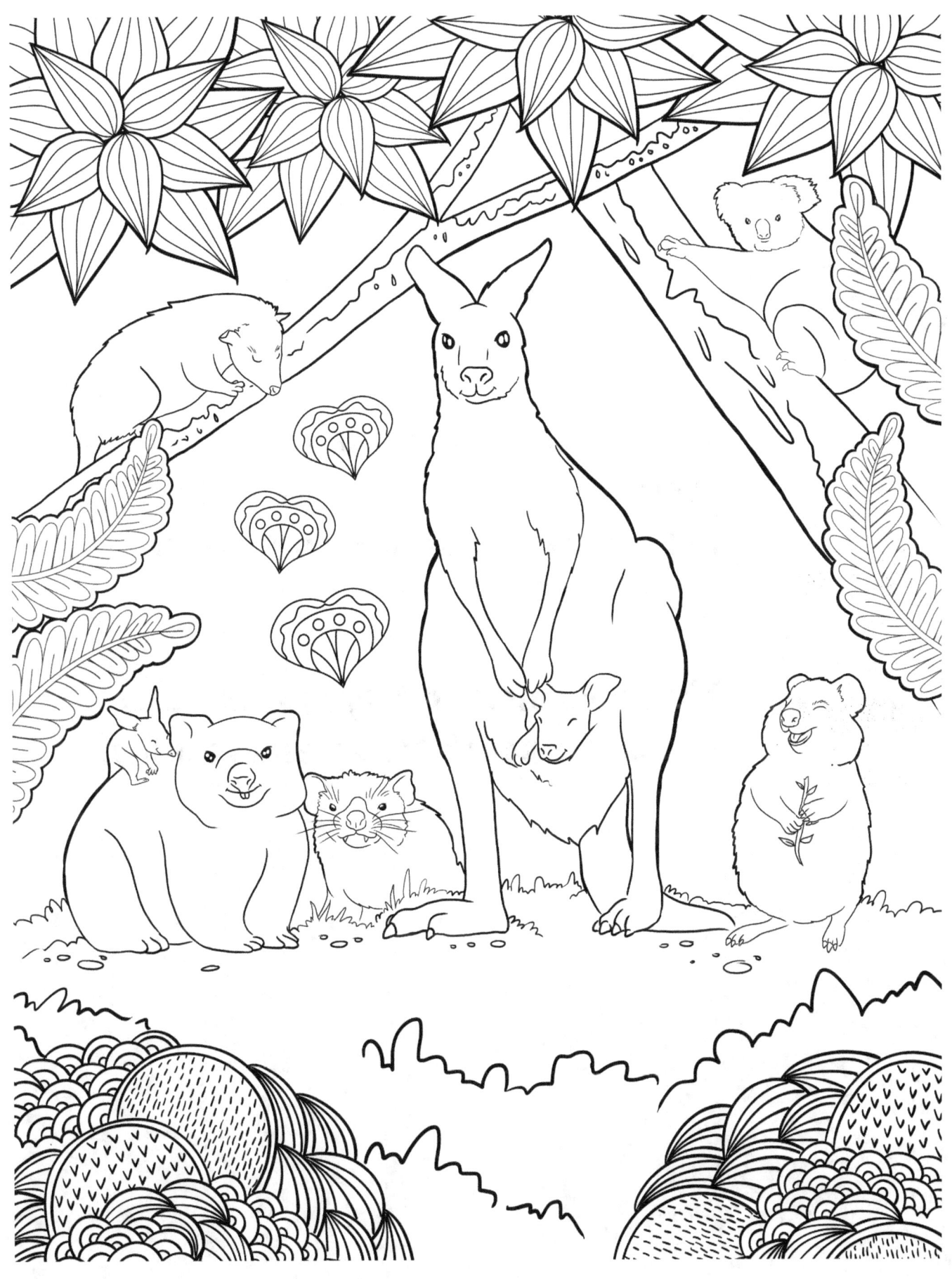

With a marsupial pouch for taking their babies around, anything is possumble for mother opossums!

They give birth to tiny "joeys" that live in the pouch for several months.

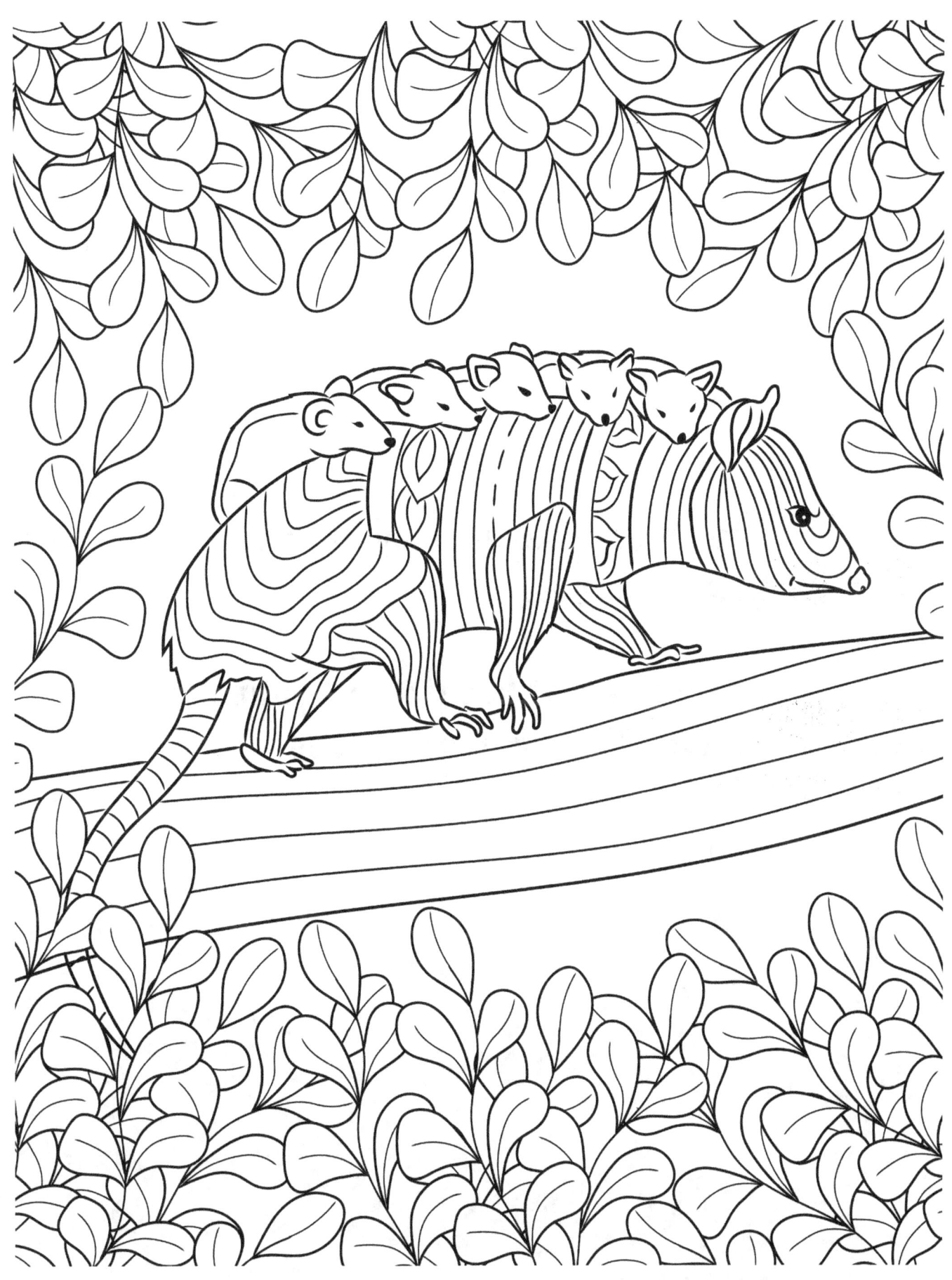

A mother opossum may have 1-3 litters per year.

While she may have 20-30 young, an average litter is 8 or 9 joeys.

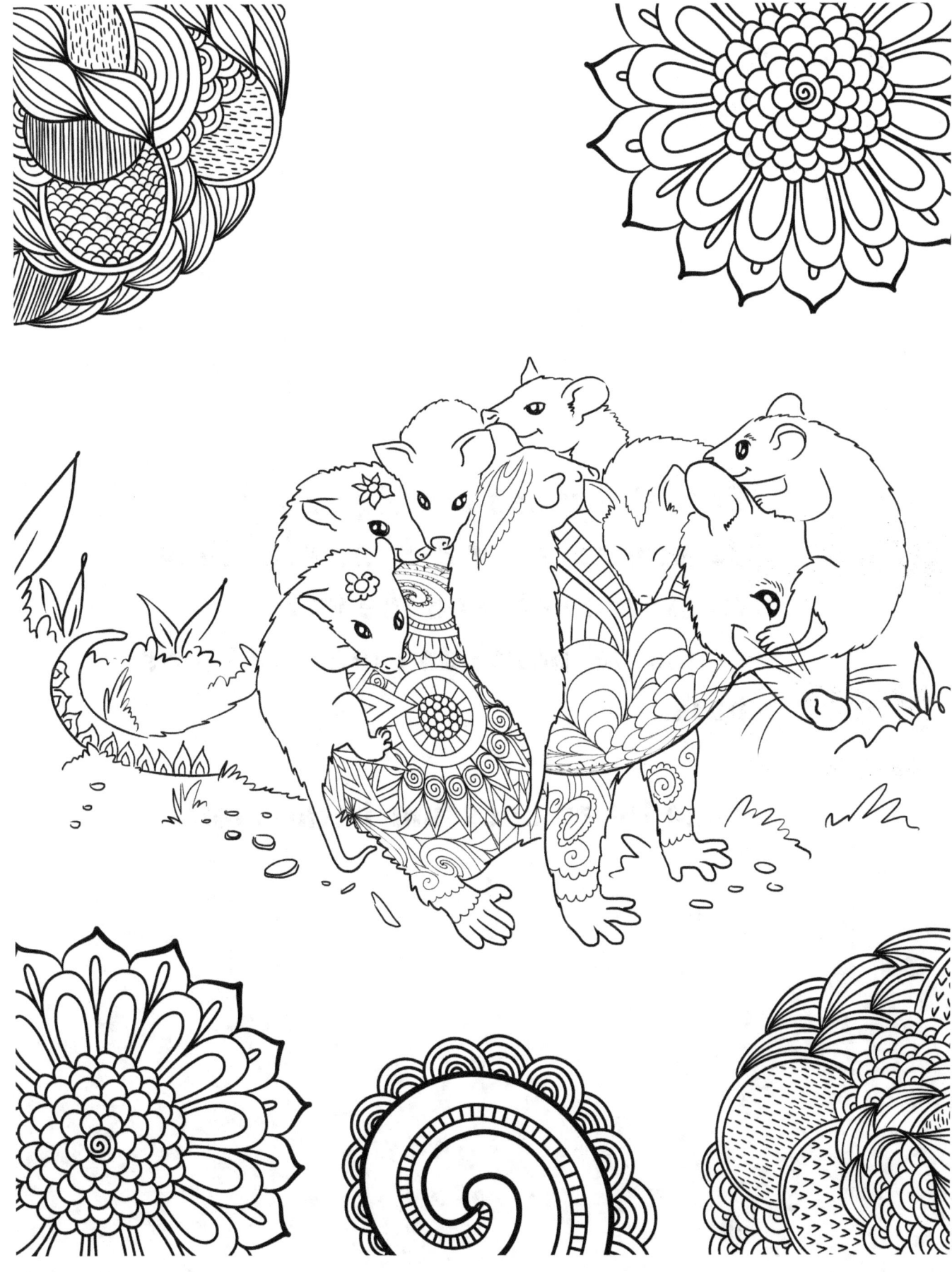

Once the young are big and more developed, after 2-3 months, they transition between the warm marsupial pouch and their mother's back.

Time for an opossum-back-ride!

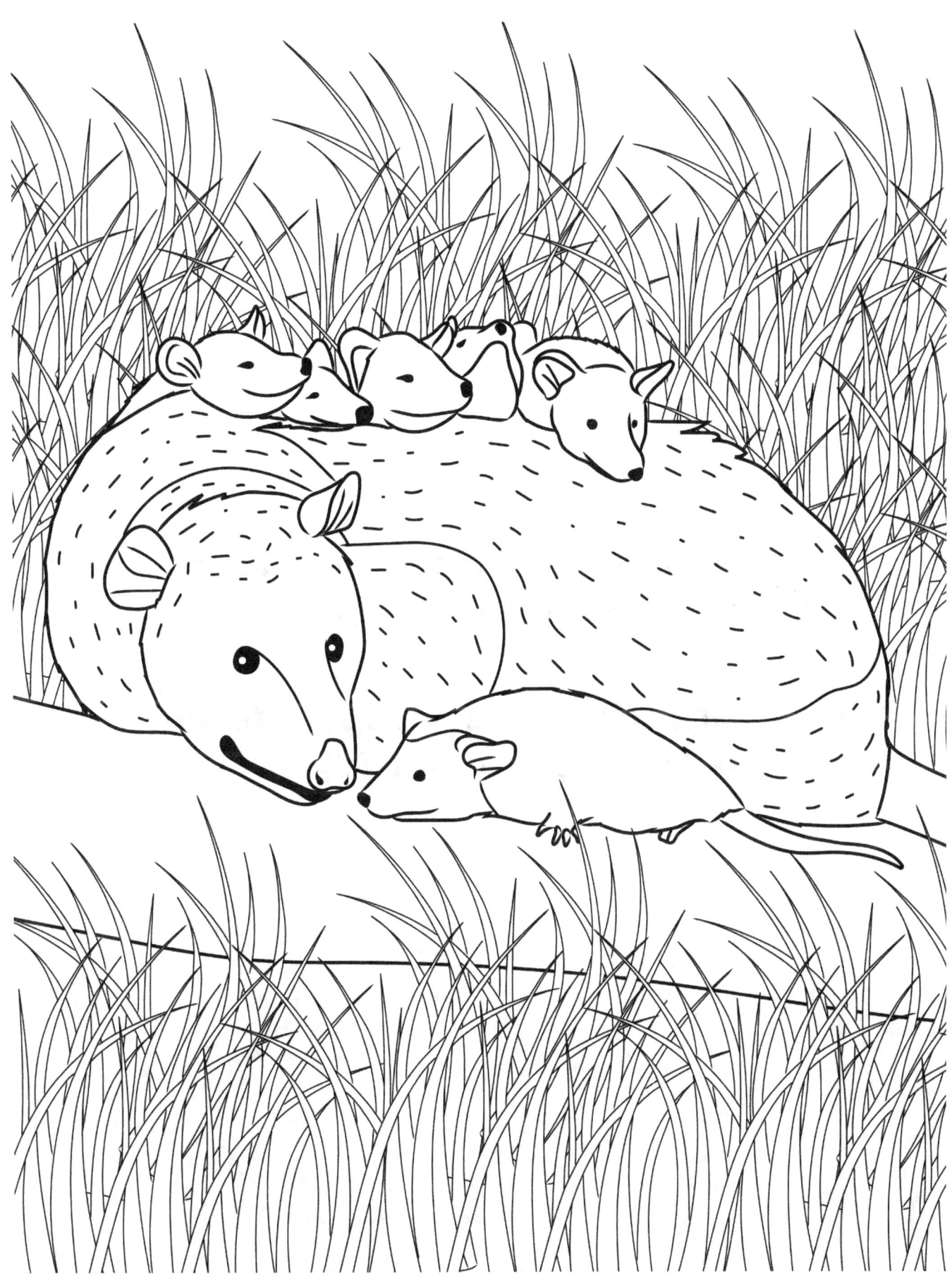

Adolescent opossums leave their mother after 4-5 months.

Later, Mom! I've got places to go and trash cans to visit!

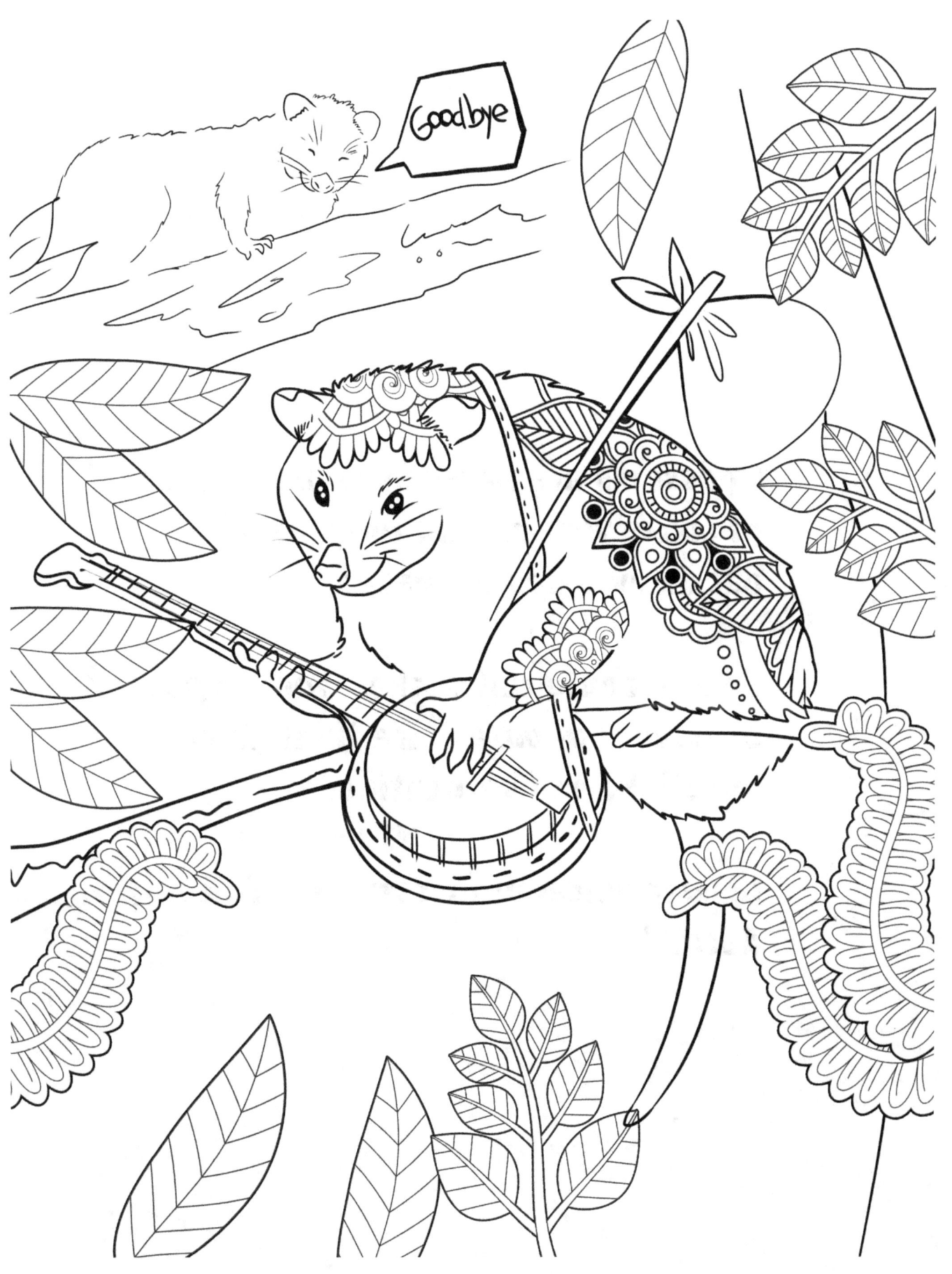

Opossums are immune to most types of snake venom, and they actually eat many types of snakes.

Some people call snakes *nope ropes* or *danger noodles*. We think they are slinky and serpentine.

Hisssteerrical or hisssstory? You decide!

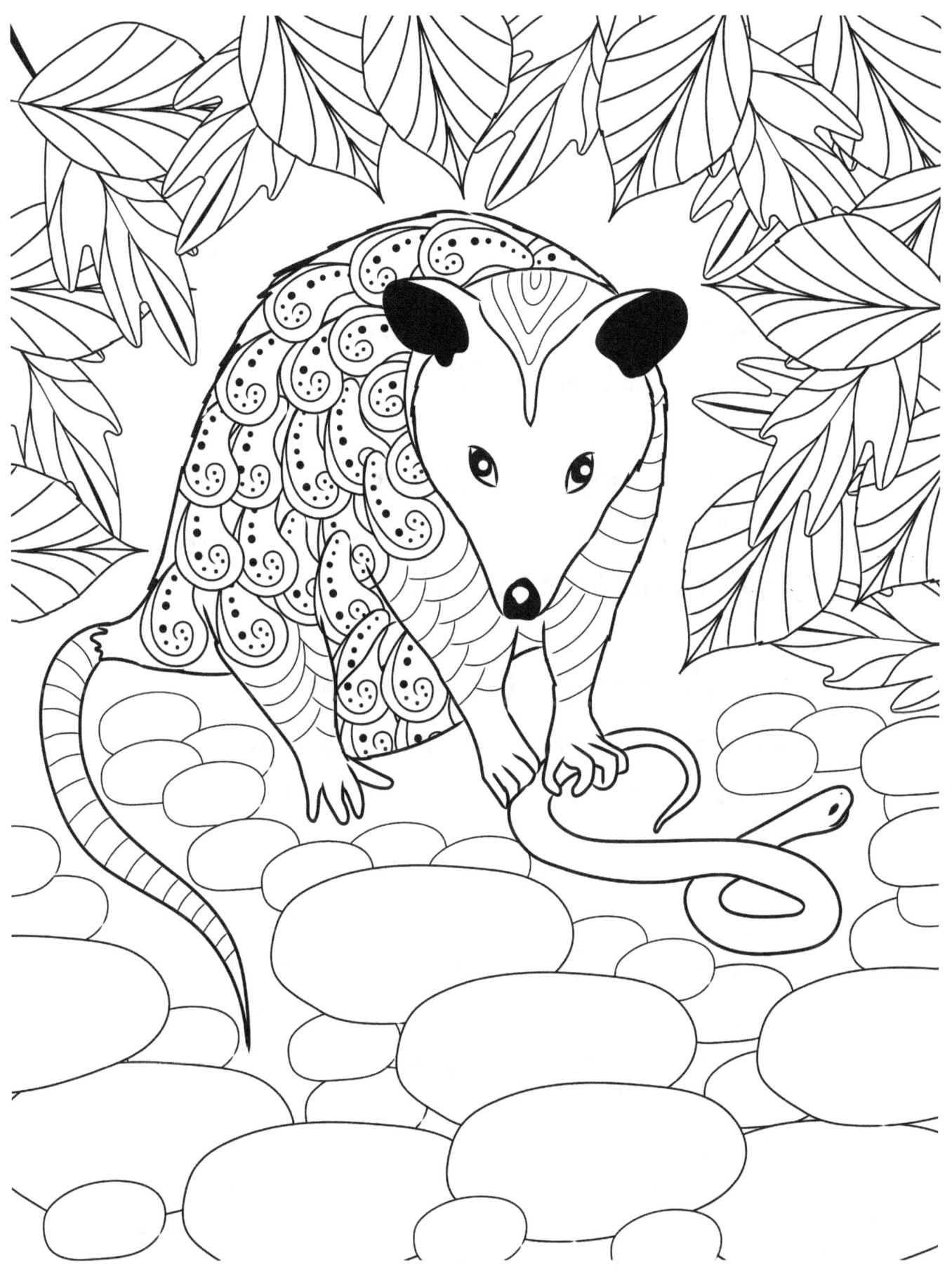

Now what's up (or down?) with that hairless rat-like tail?

That's actually a prehensile tail! Prehensile tails are used like an extra limb to grab or hold things.

The word stems from the Latin *prehendere*, which means *to take hold of or grasp*.

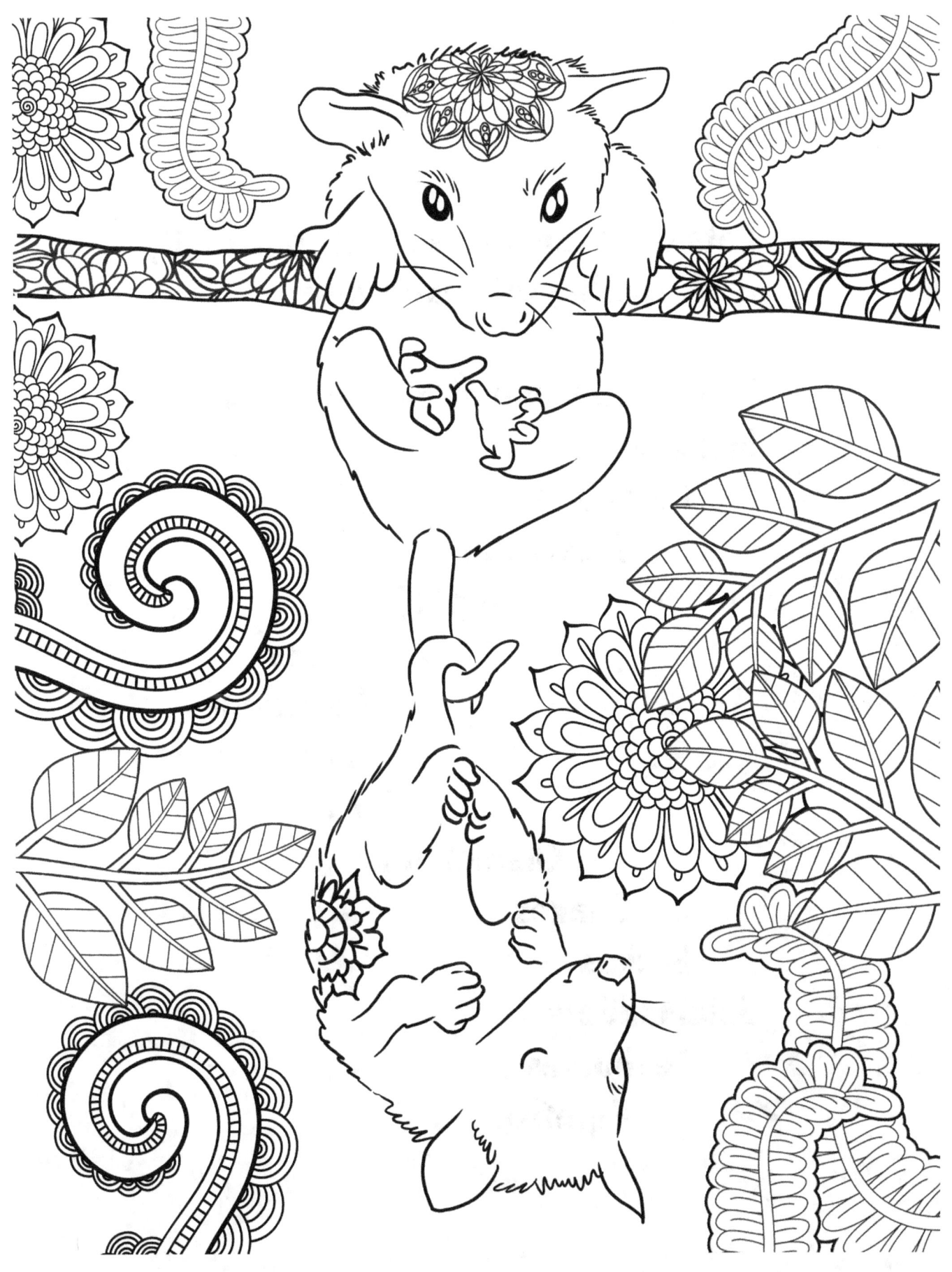

Lots of other cool animals have fully or partially prehensile tails.

These are some of our favorites:
Monkeys
    Anteaters
        Binturong
            Kinkajou
                Pangolins
                    Porcupines
                  Rats
              Skinks
          Chameleons
        Snakes
      Geckos
    Salamanders
      Seahorses
        Pipefish

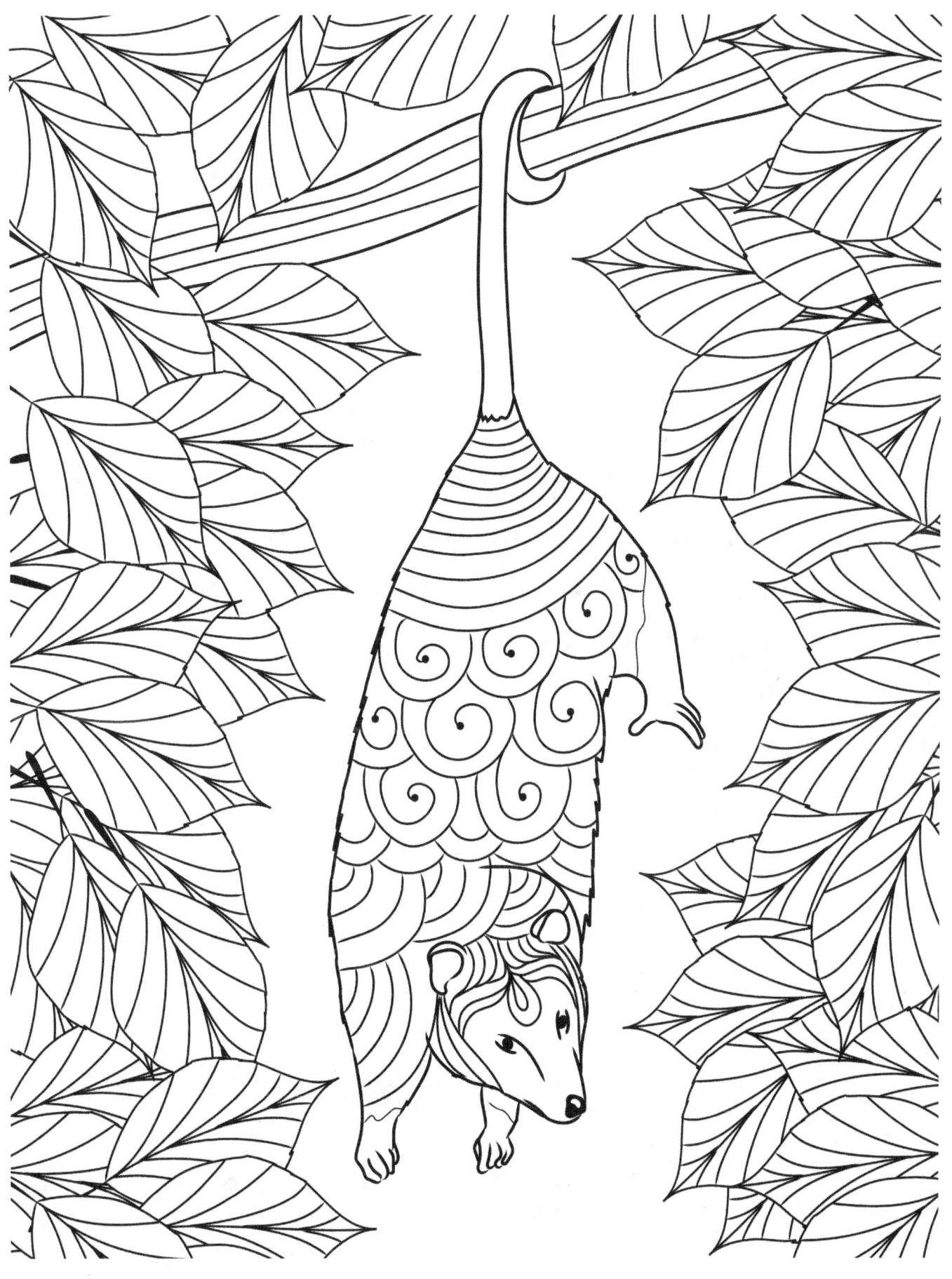

Opossums use the prehensile tails to grip trees they are climbing, carry materials for building nests, and even hang from branches (when they are tiny and *extra* cute!).

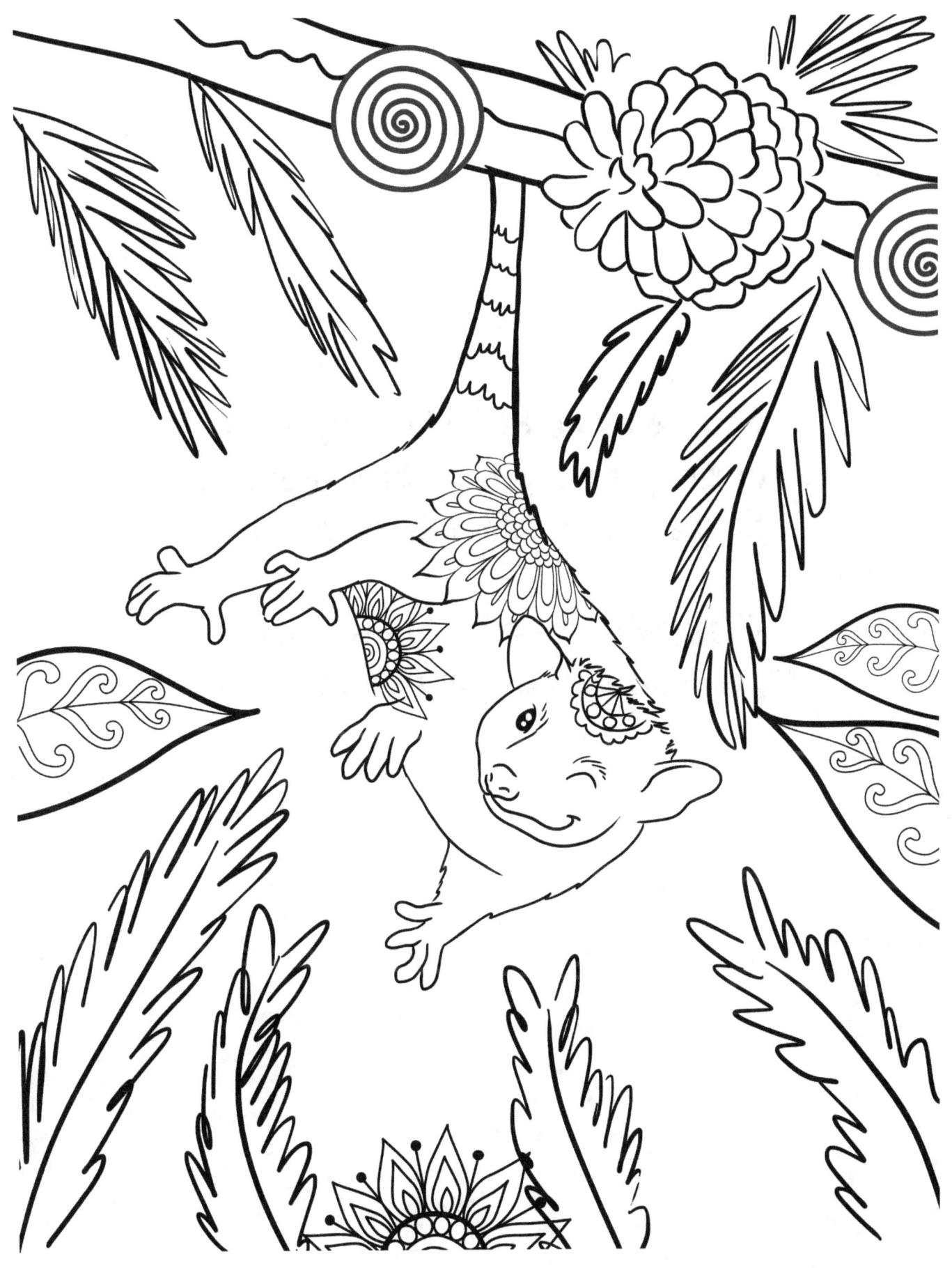

Opossums do NOT sleep upside-down (hanging from branches) as they are often seen in cartoons.

Their tails are mighty awesome possum, but they aren't that strong.

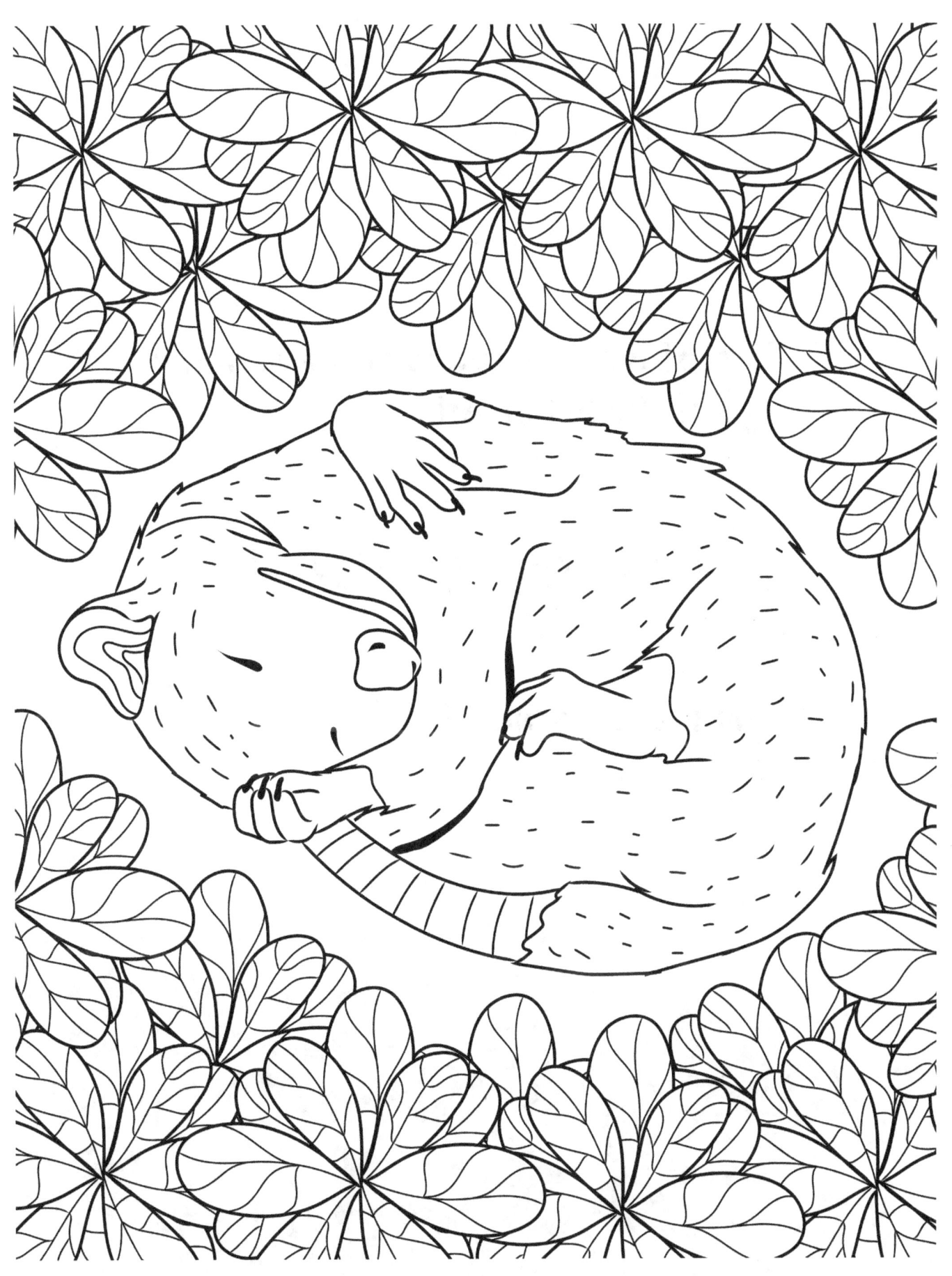

Part of the opossum's allure is in the eye of the beholder!

Their eyes appear almost jet-black.

Any eye-deas why?

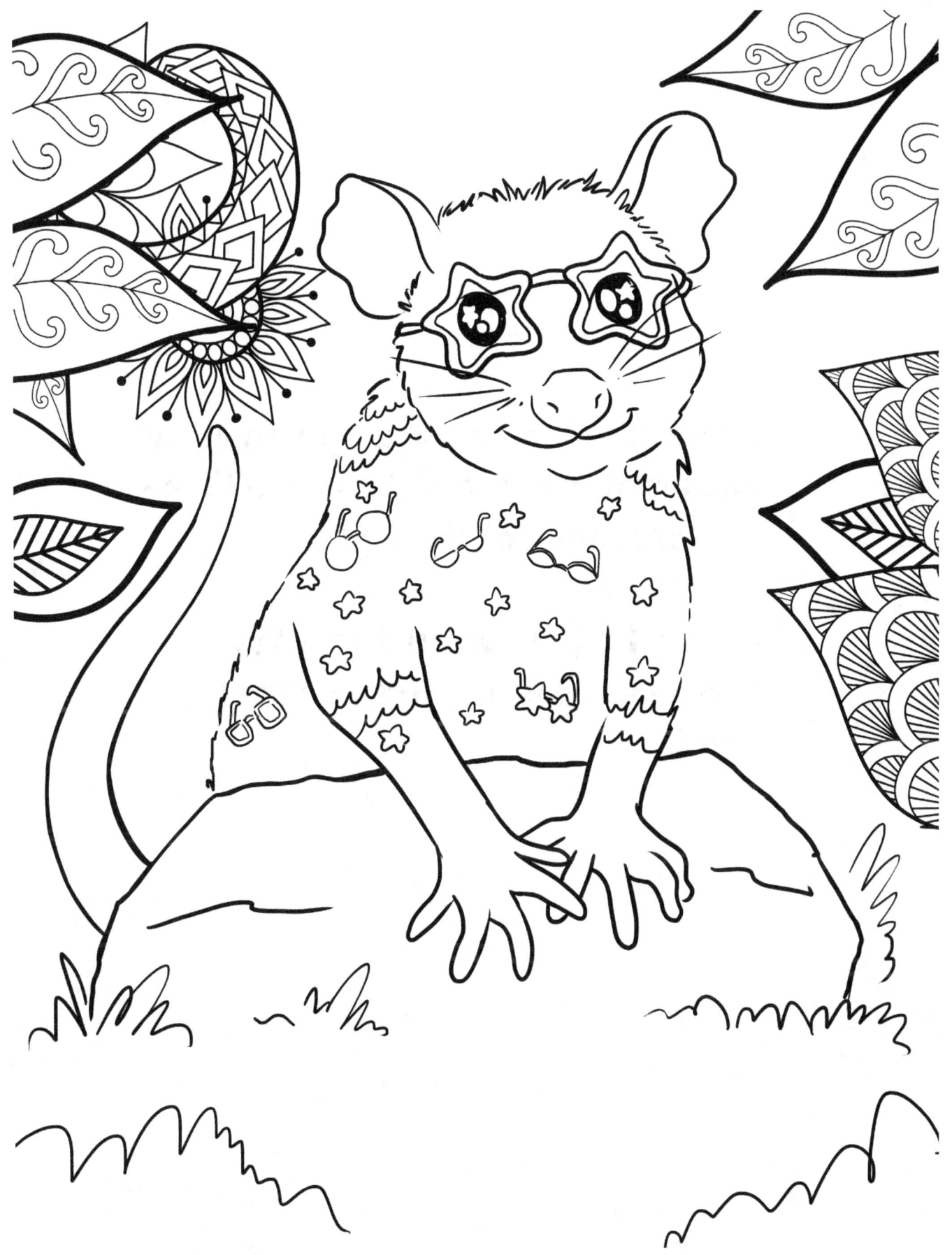

If you said it's because opossums are nocturnal, you are right -- like these *cool* creatures of the night!

Having large pupils is thought to allow the opossum to see better at night.

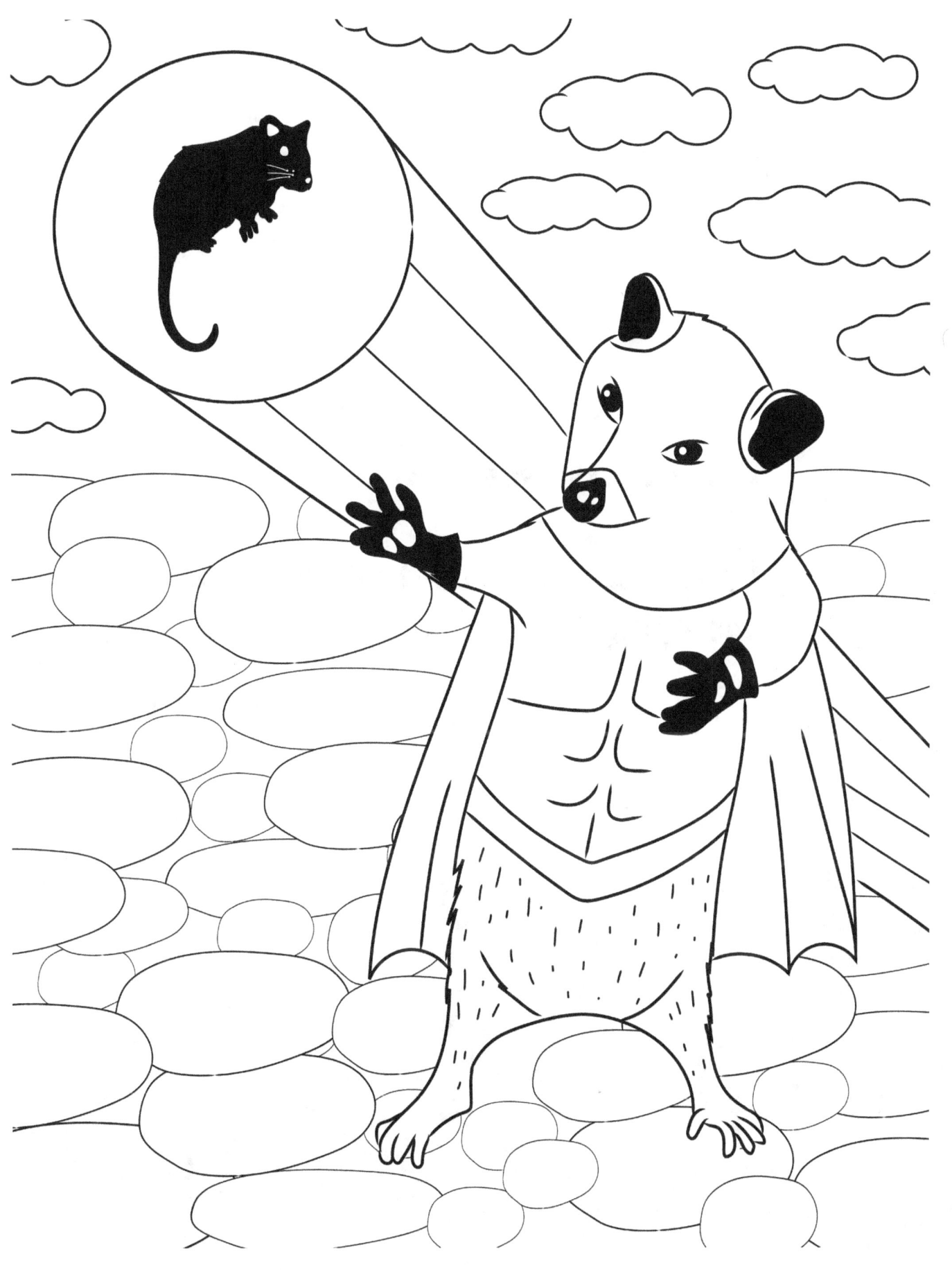

Brace yourselves!

Opossums have about 50 teeth for chomping.

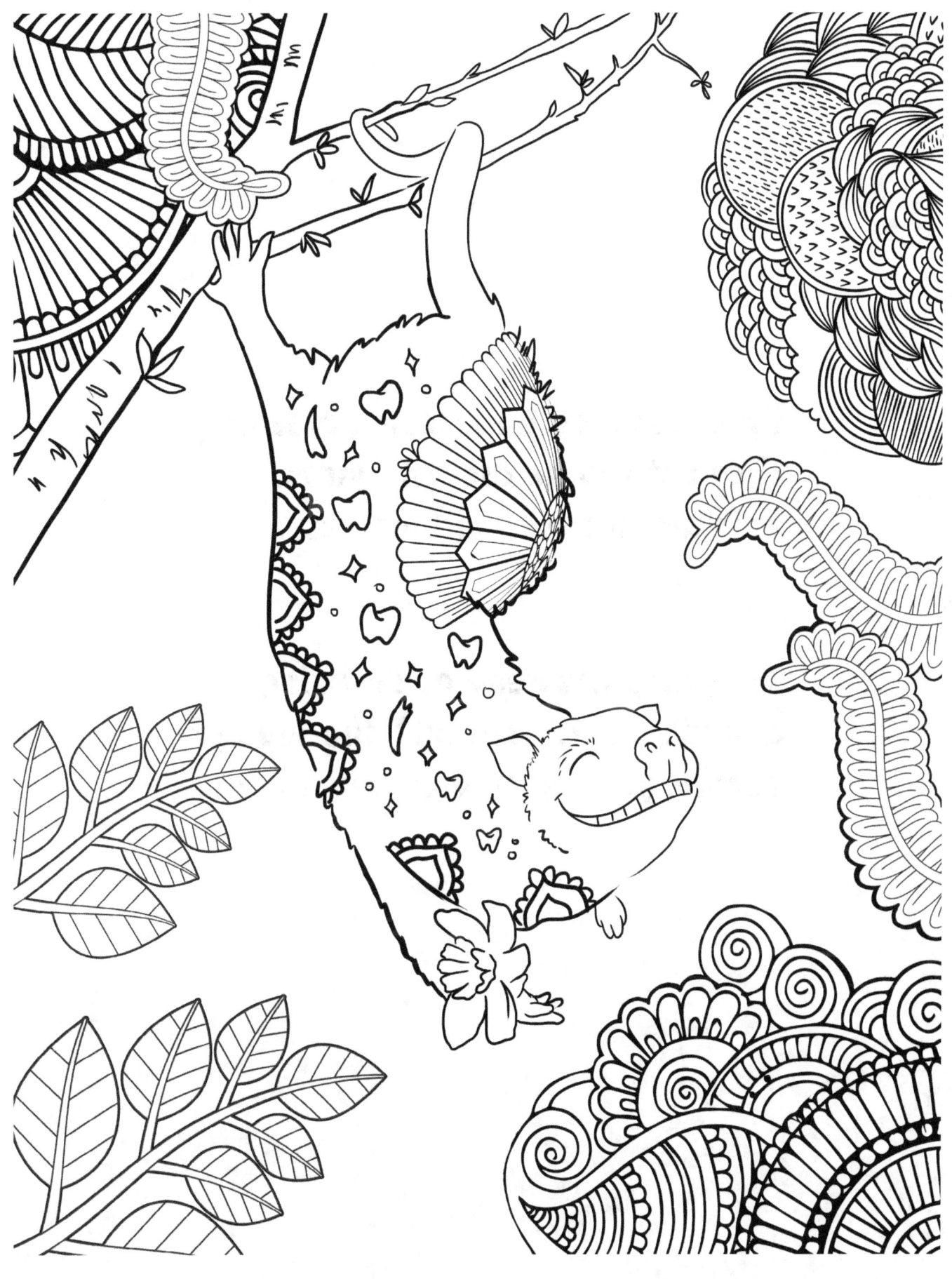

Opossums are omnivores, meaning they eat a wide diet of plants, animals, worms, and insects.

They also eat dead or decaying animals, which are NOT the type of *carrion* you would bring on a trip!

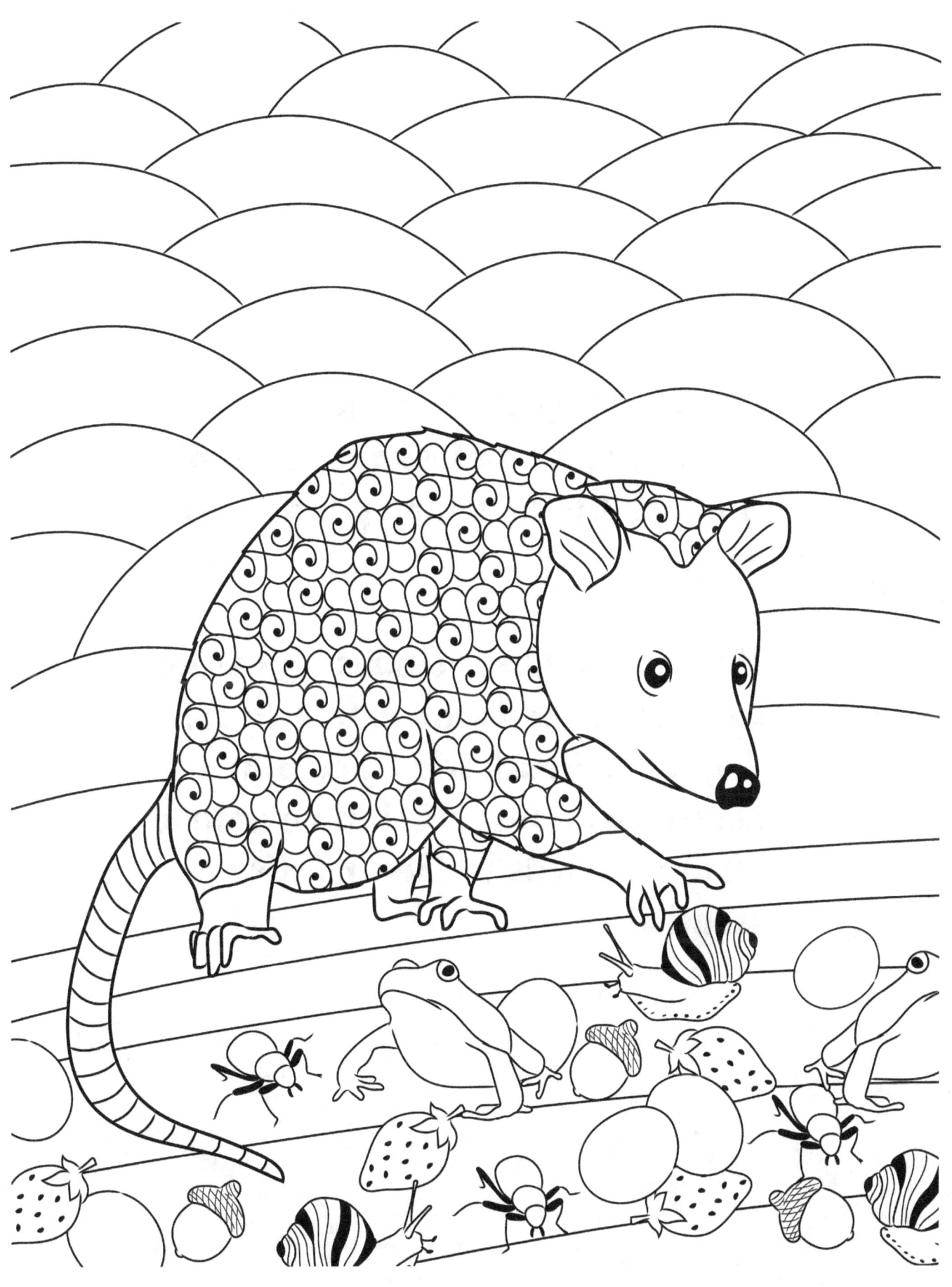

Part of the opossum's success in settled areas and living near people is the ability to be an opportunistic eater.

This means, like raccoons, opossums sometimes are found eating trash, dog food, French fries, and other human creations. Their time around trash cans adds to their mystical scent!

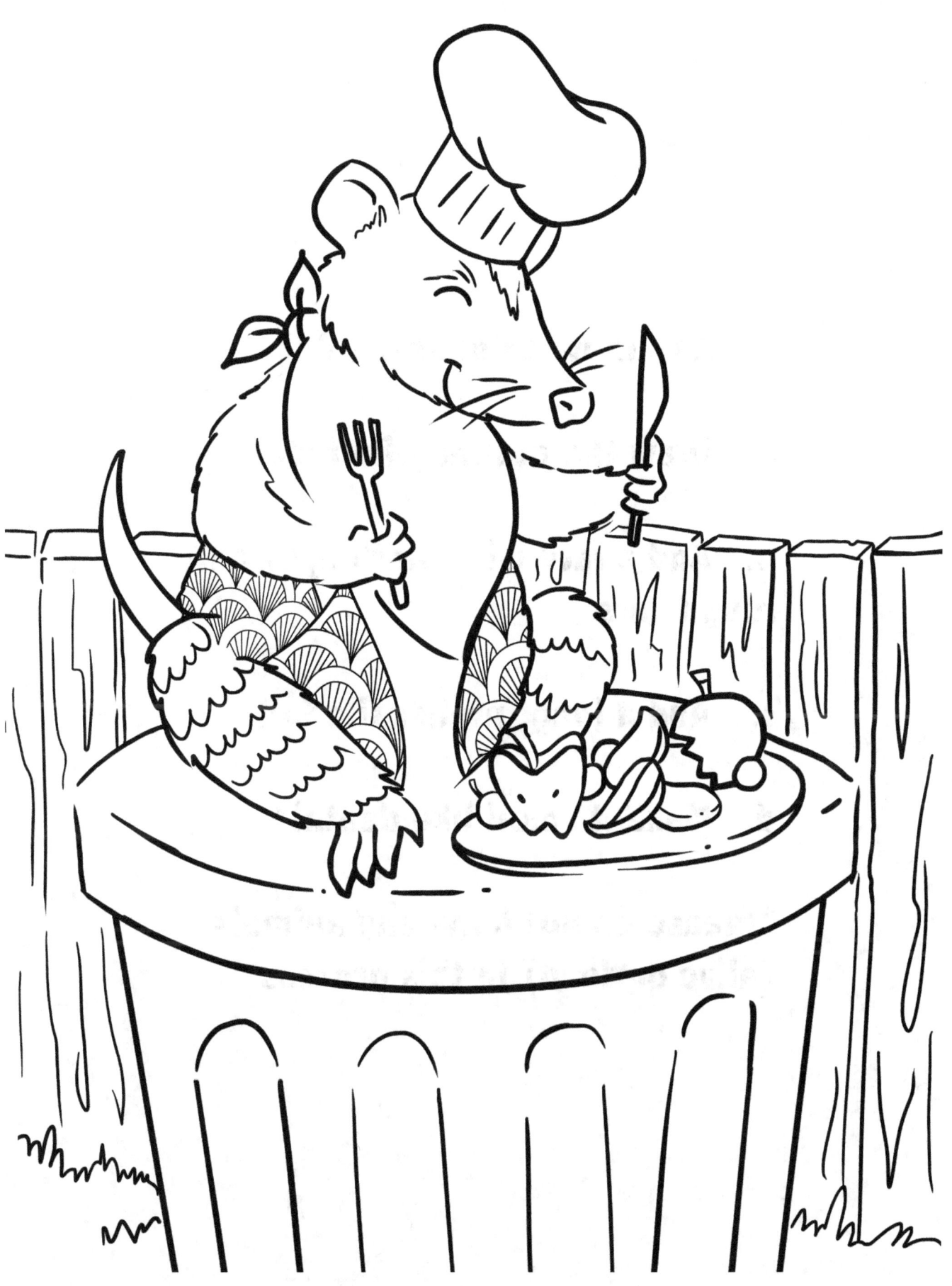

Want to draw an opossum?

a. Draw the outline of a rat

b. Add a face with black eyes and round ears

c. Add a long, prehensile tail

d. Make it smell like death!*

*Please do not harm any animals (alive or dead) in this process

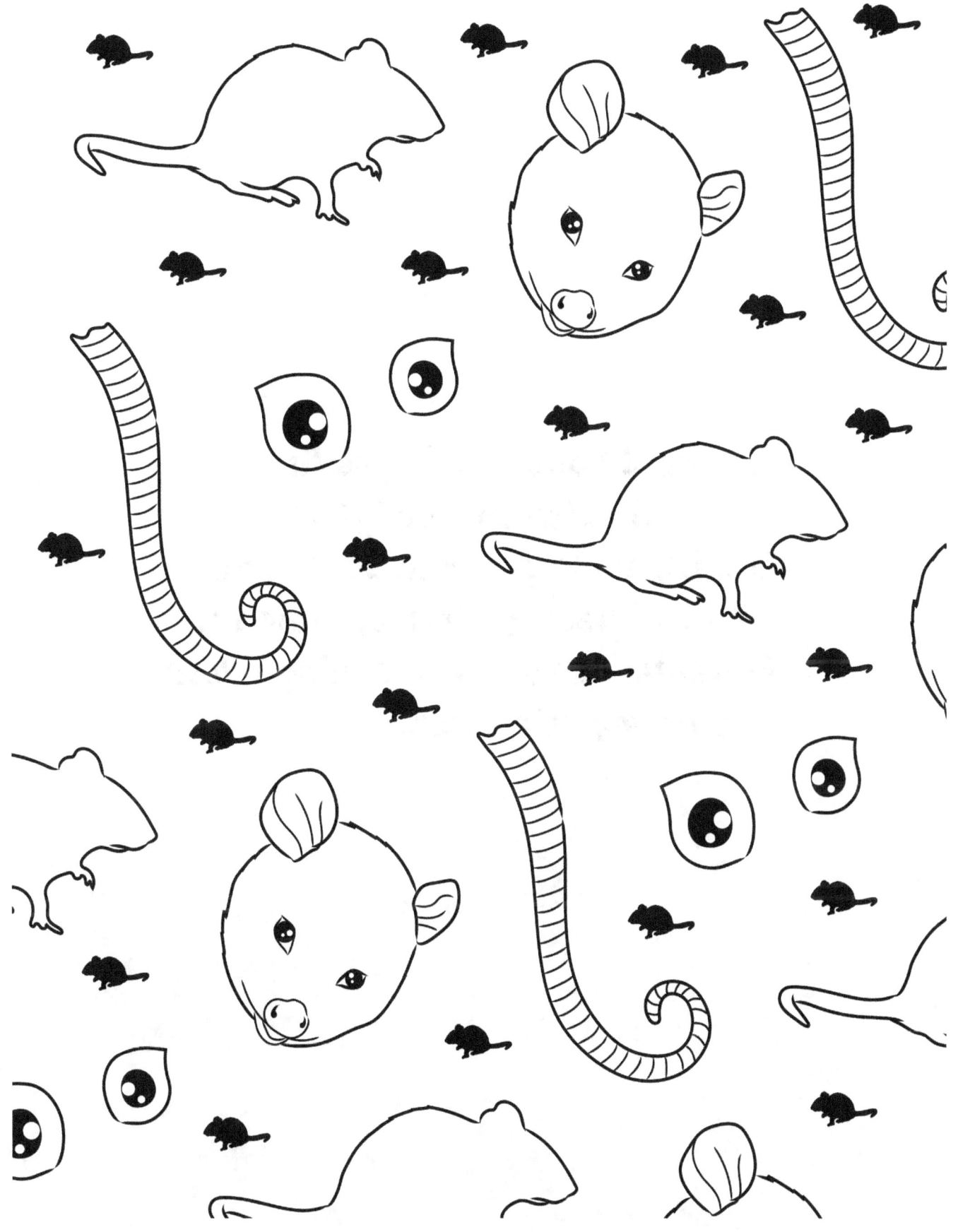

The word "opossum" was first recorded between 1607-1611 by English explorers John Smith and William Strachey, derived from the Powhatan language, meaning *white dog or dog-like beast*.

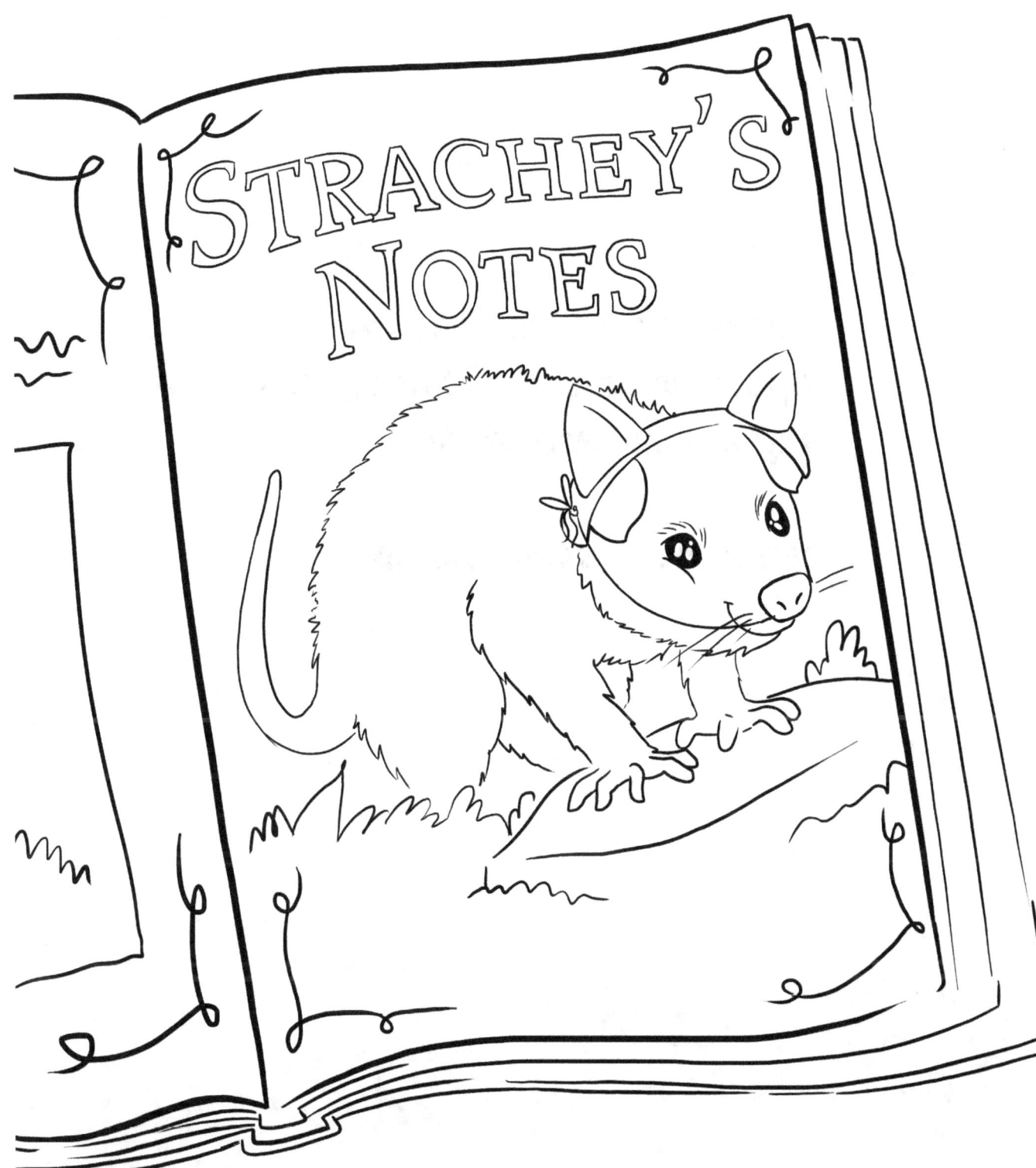

Strachey's notes describe the opossum as a *beast in bigness of a pig and in taste alike*.

We're not *bacon* this up!

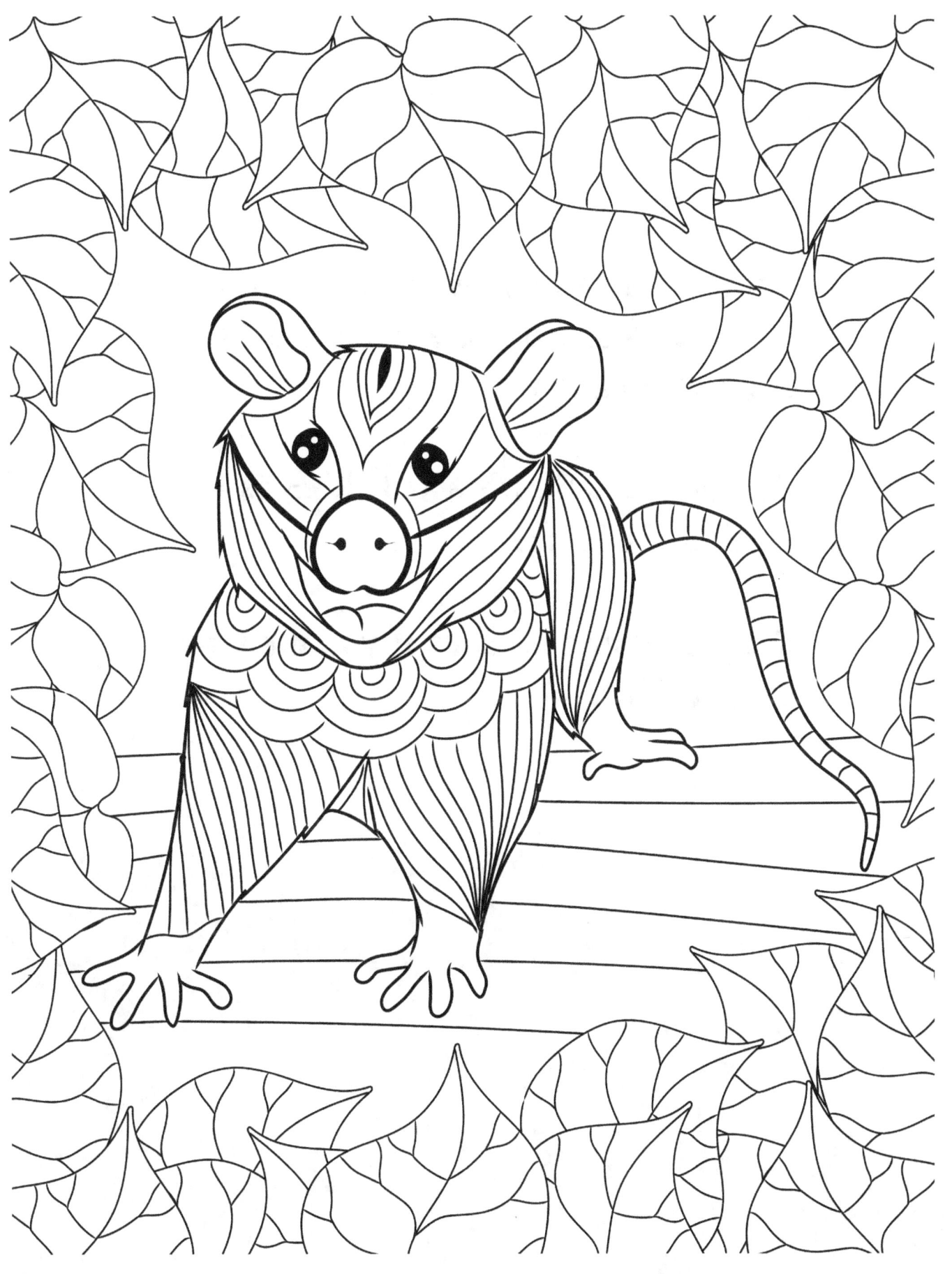

Smith said the opossum *has a head like a swine...tail like a rat...of the bigness of a cat.*

Do you think Smith was telling the truth or fe-lying?

It's just swine with us if you meow-s over it a bit.

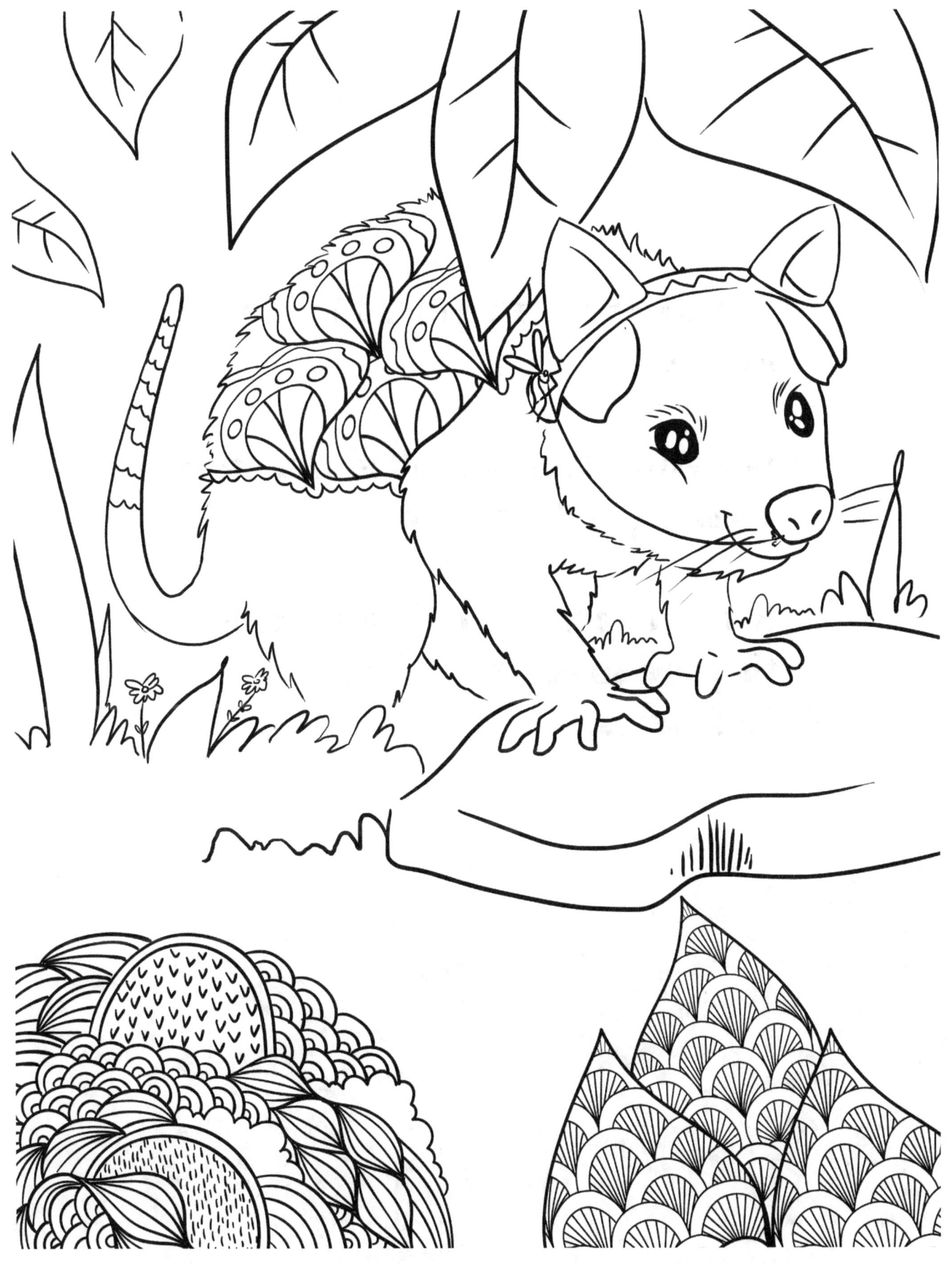

Opossums are also found in Central America.

In Mexico, they are called *tlacuache*, *tacuachi*, and *tlacuachi*.

In other Spanish-speaking countries, they are sometimes called *zarigüeyas*.

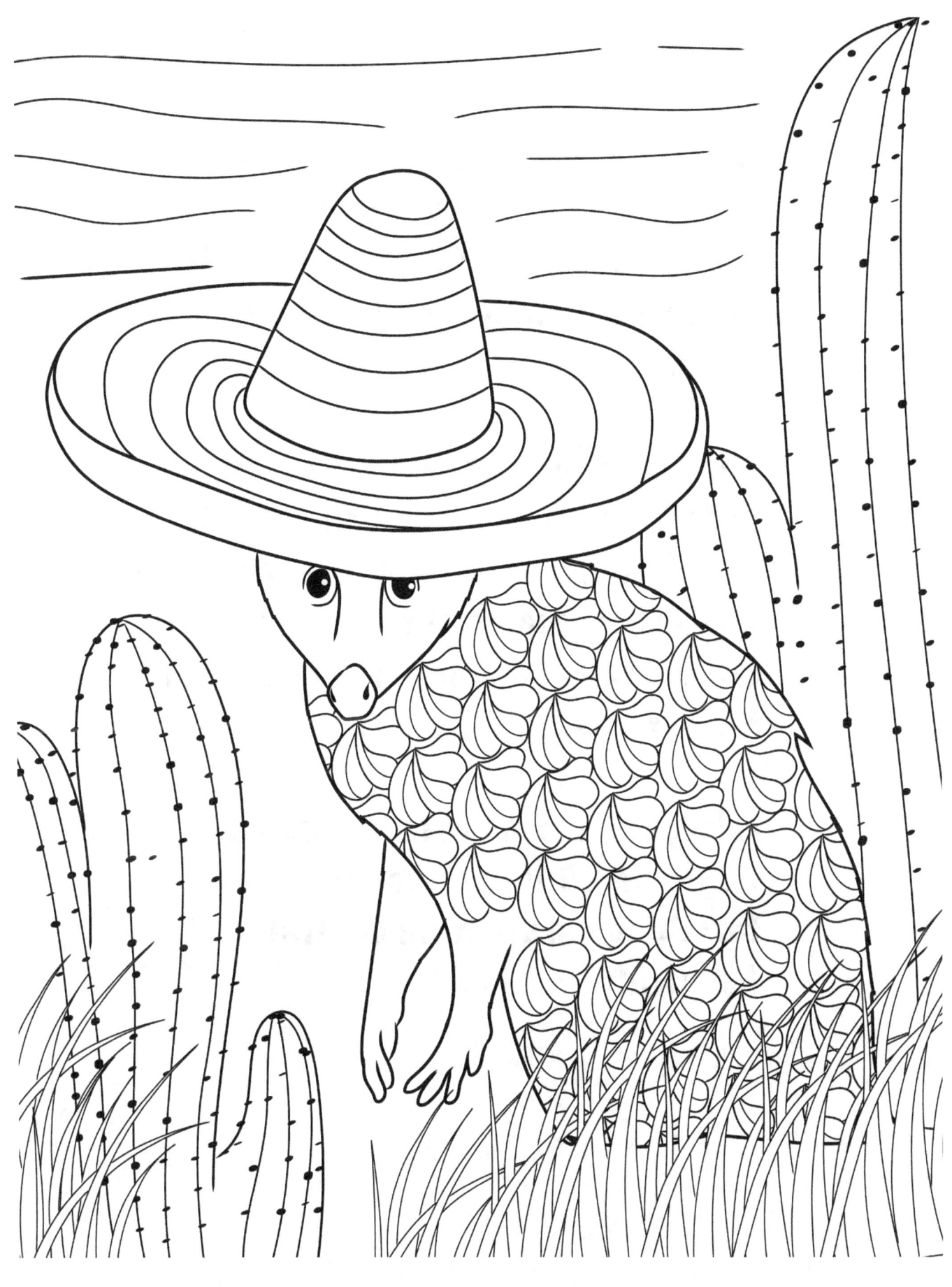

Opossums are about the size of a house cat, with larger animals being found further to the north of their range and smaller ones near the equator.

They measure about 13-37 inches (35-94 cm) from snout to the tail base and weigh 1.7-14 pounds (0.8-6.4 kg) for males and from 11 ounces to 8.2 pounds (0.3 - 3.7 kg) for females.

A large Canadian male opossum might be 20 times the size of a female opossum from Central America!

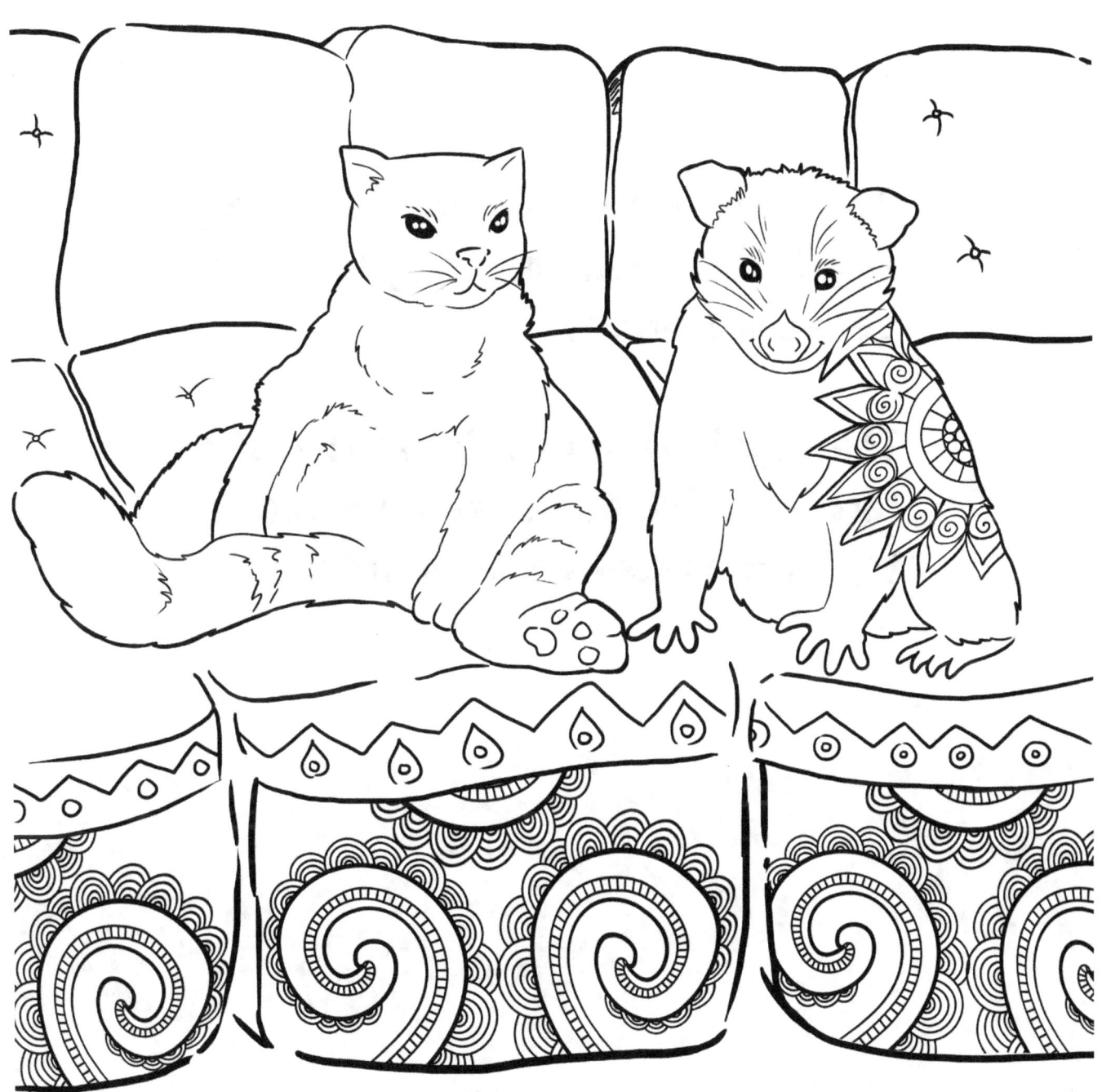

Opossums are considered to be very smart, often remembering locations between seasons.

Their brain is one-fifth the size of a racoon's. We do not recommend trying to measure this yourself.

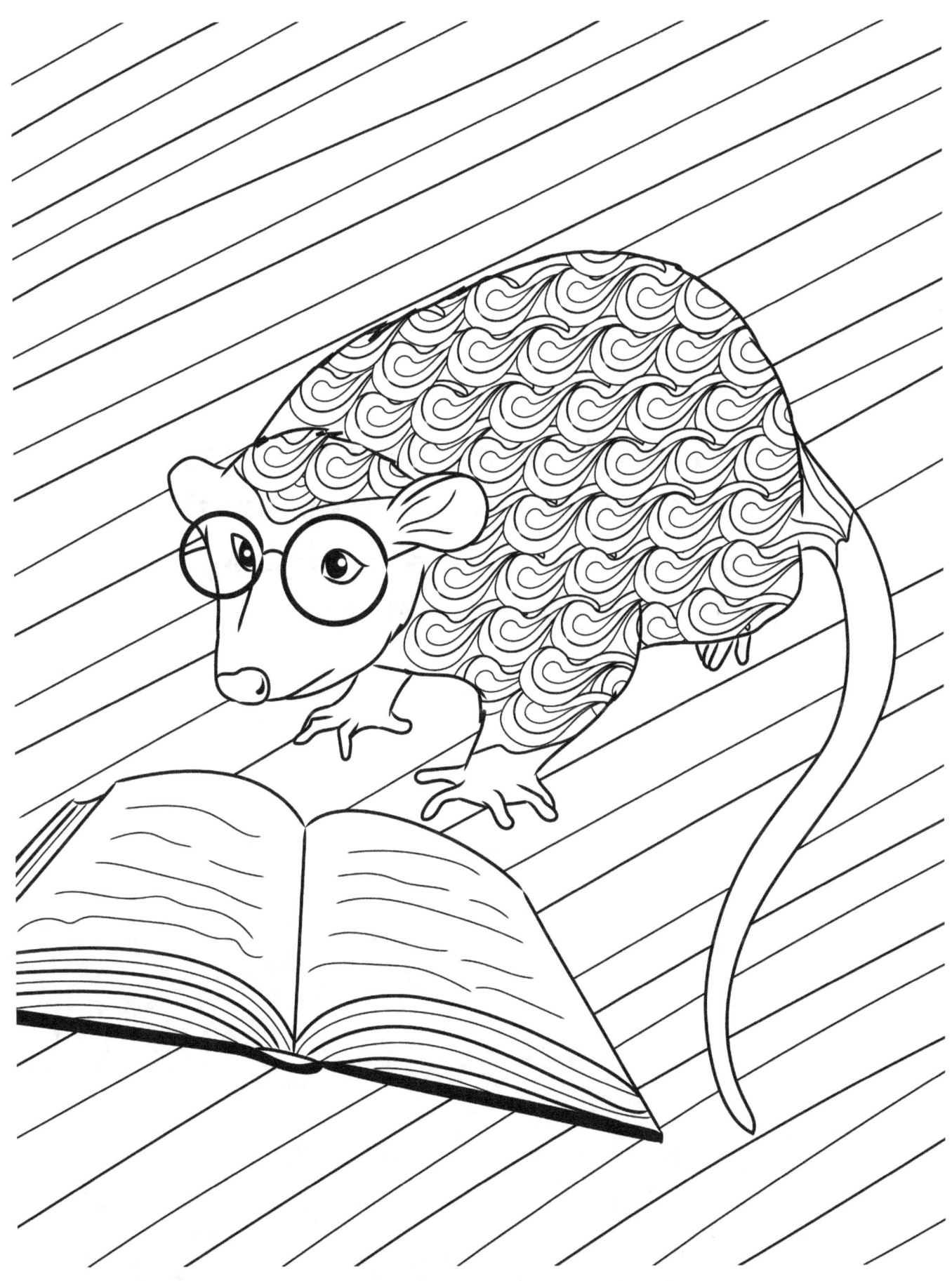

Opossums have five claws per paw, and their back paws have opposable "thumbs" that help with climbing and sending text messages.

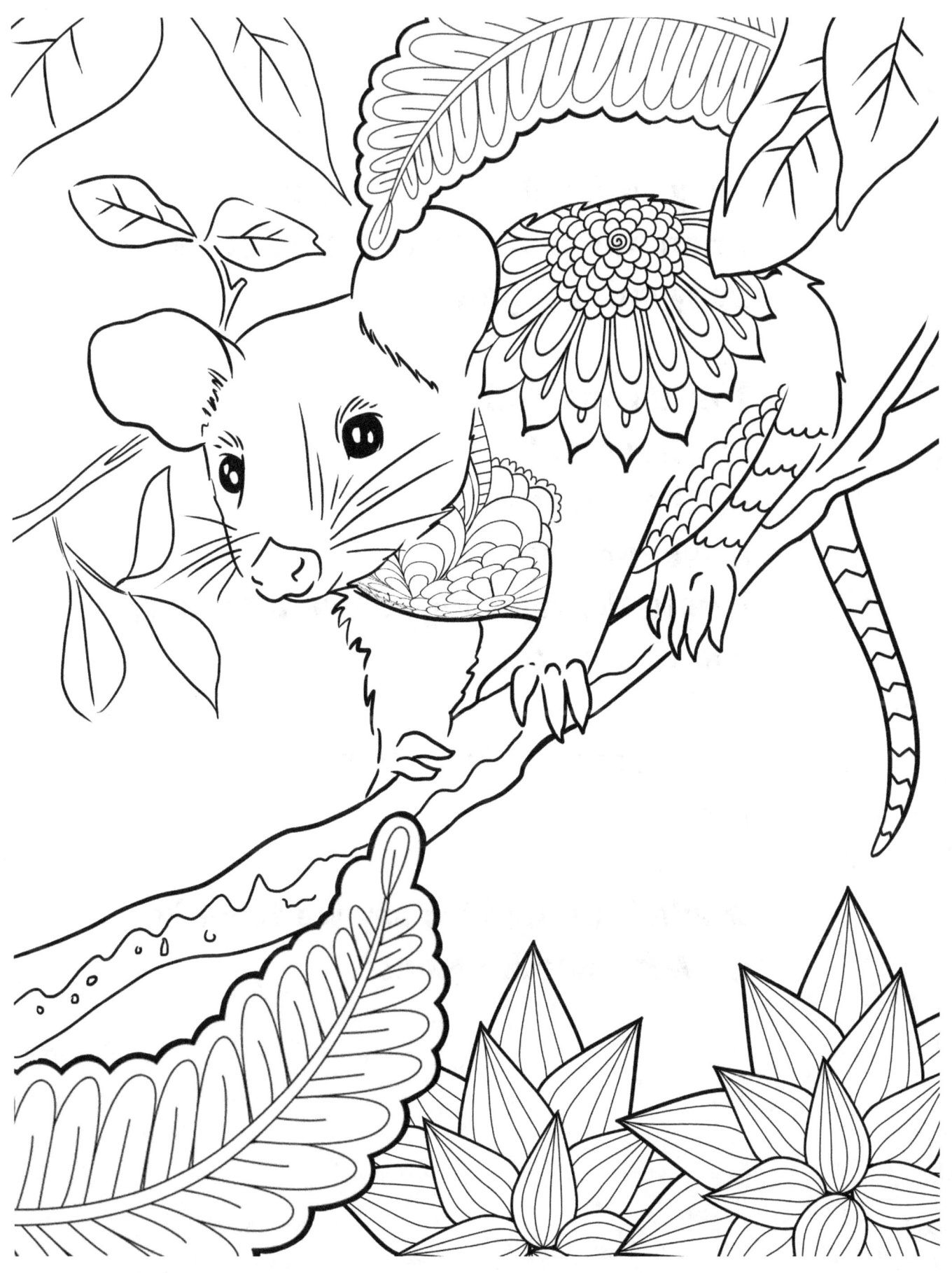

They walk with a "pacing gait," where the limbs on one side of the body move together.

This means their
left front and
left back legs
move together
before the right legs move together,
and vice/versa.

This changes when the opossum runs.

Would it be *right* to say we feel like we *left* something out?

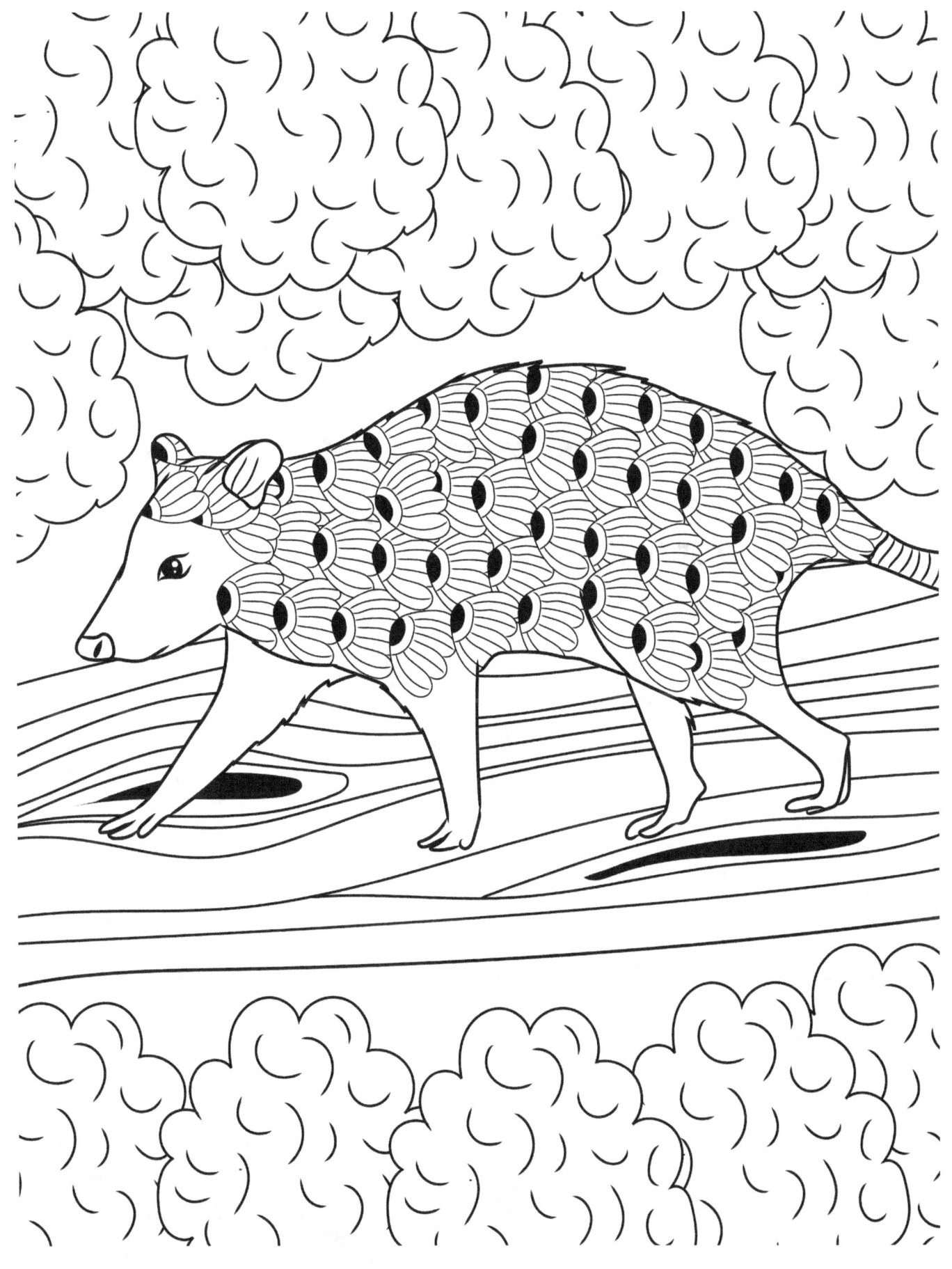

Opossums live for about 2 years in the wild and up to 4 years in captivity.

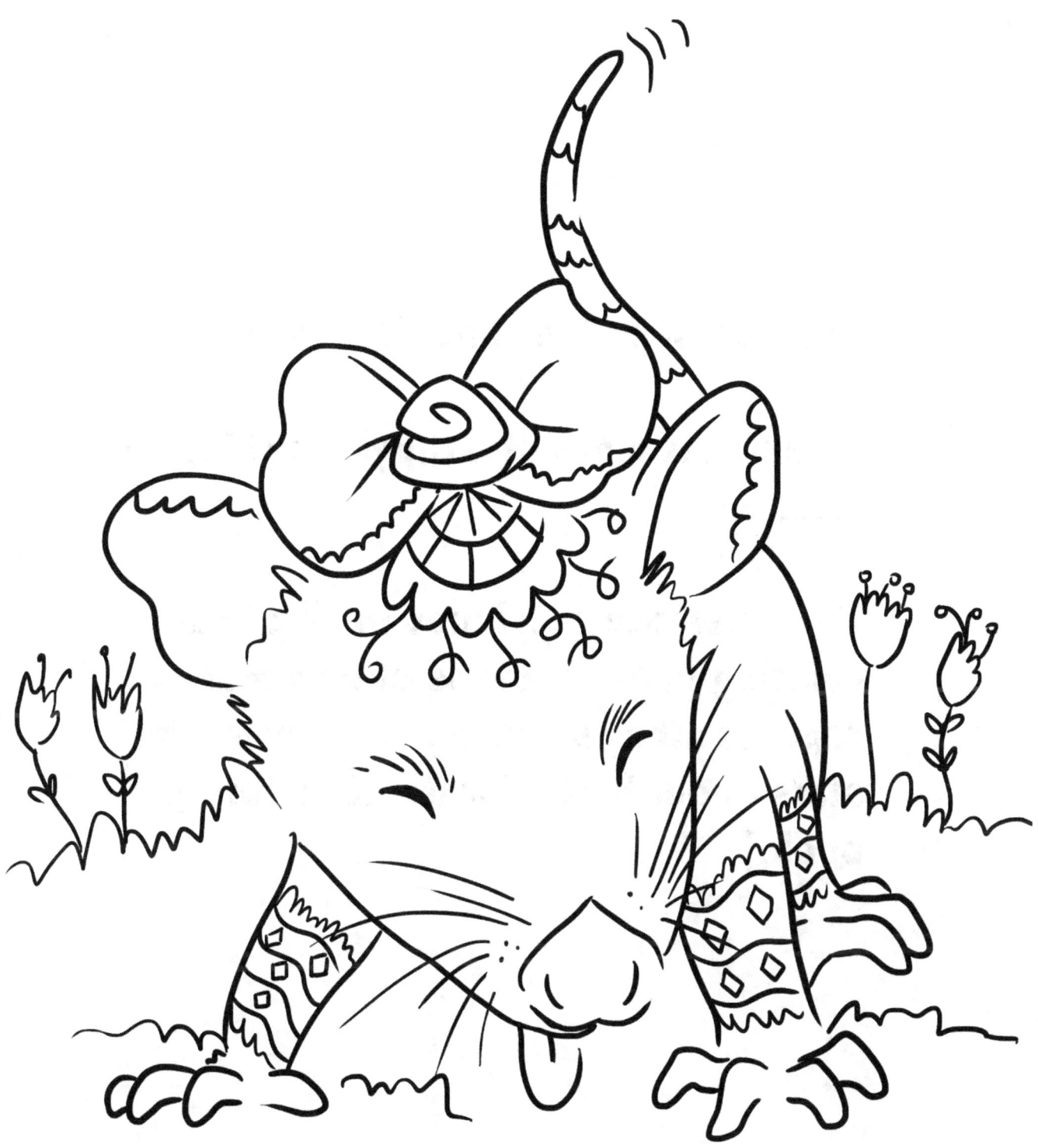

The opossum does not hibernate.

Relaxing is more of a capybara skill, after all.

[We reference capybaras in all of our coloring books because of how much capyness they bring us! They were the stars of our first educational coloring book.]

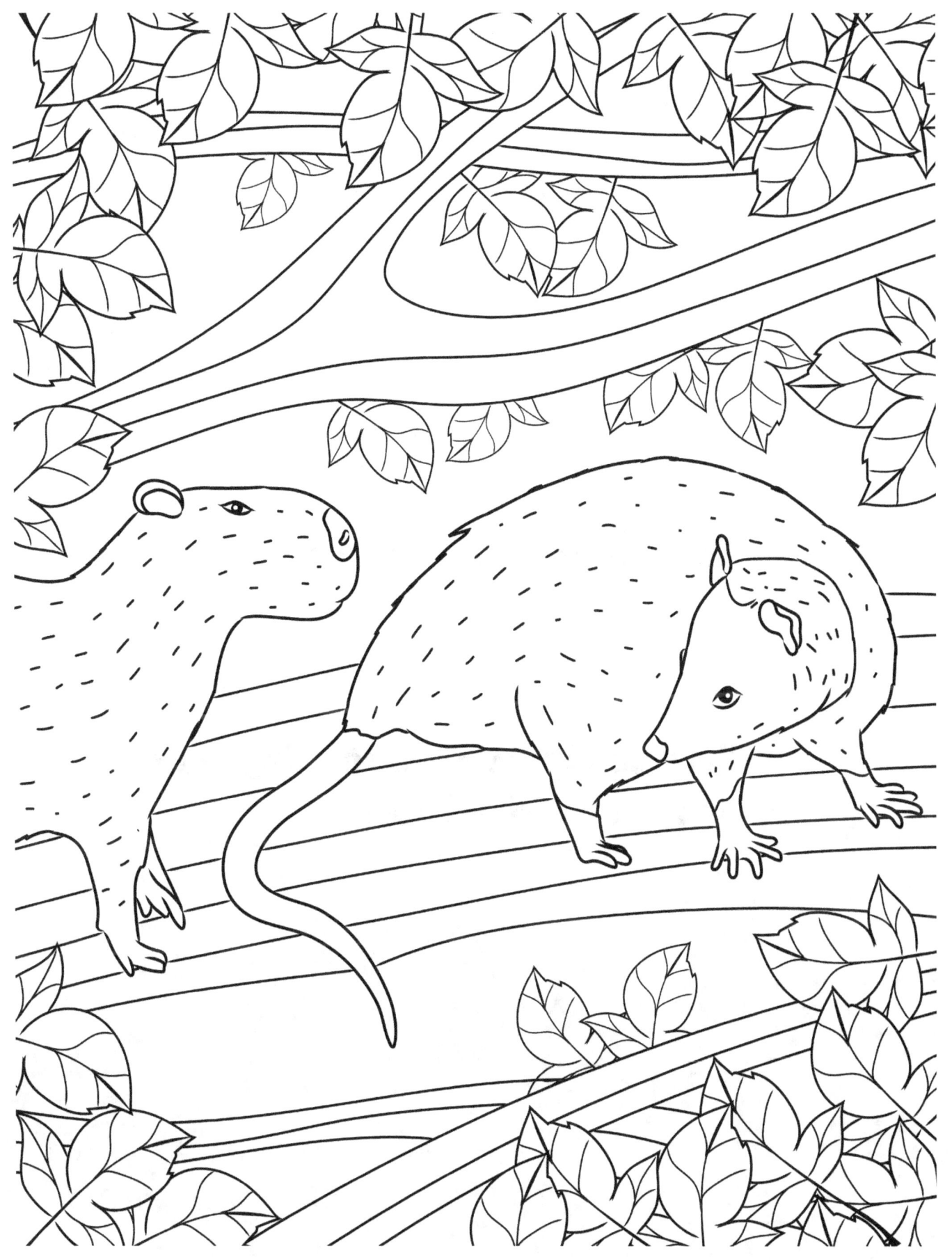

Some people eat opossum.

Fortunately, this is a coloring book and not a recipe book!

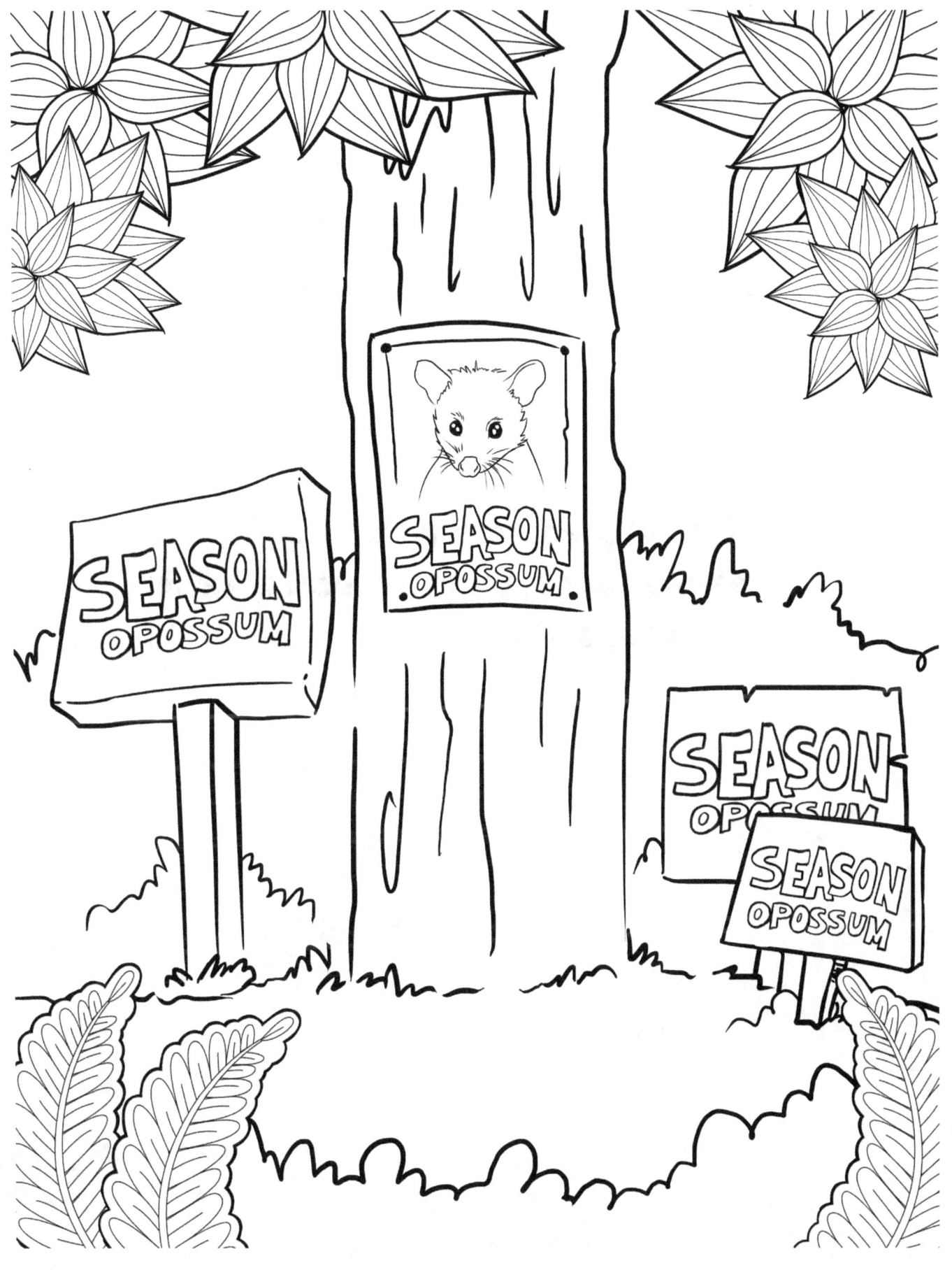

Natural predators include owls, eagles, dogs, foxes, bobcats, hawks, racoons, and cats.

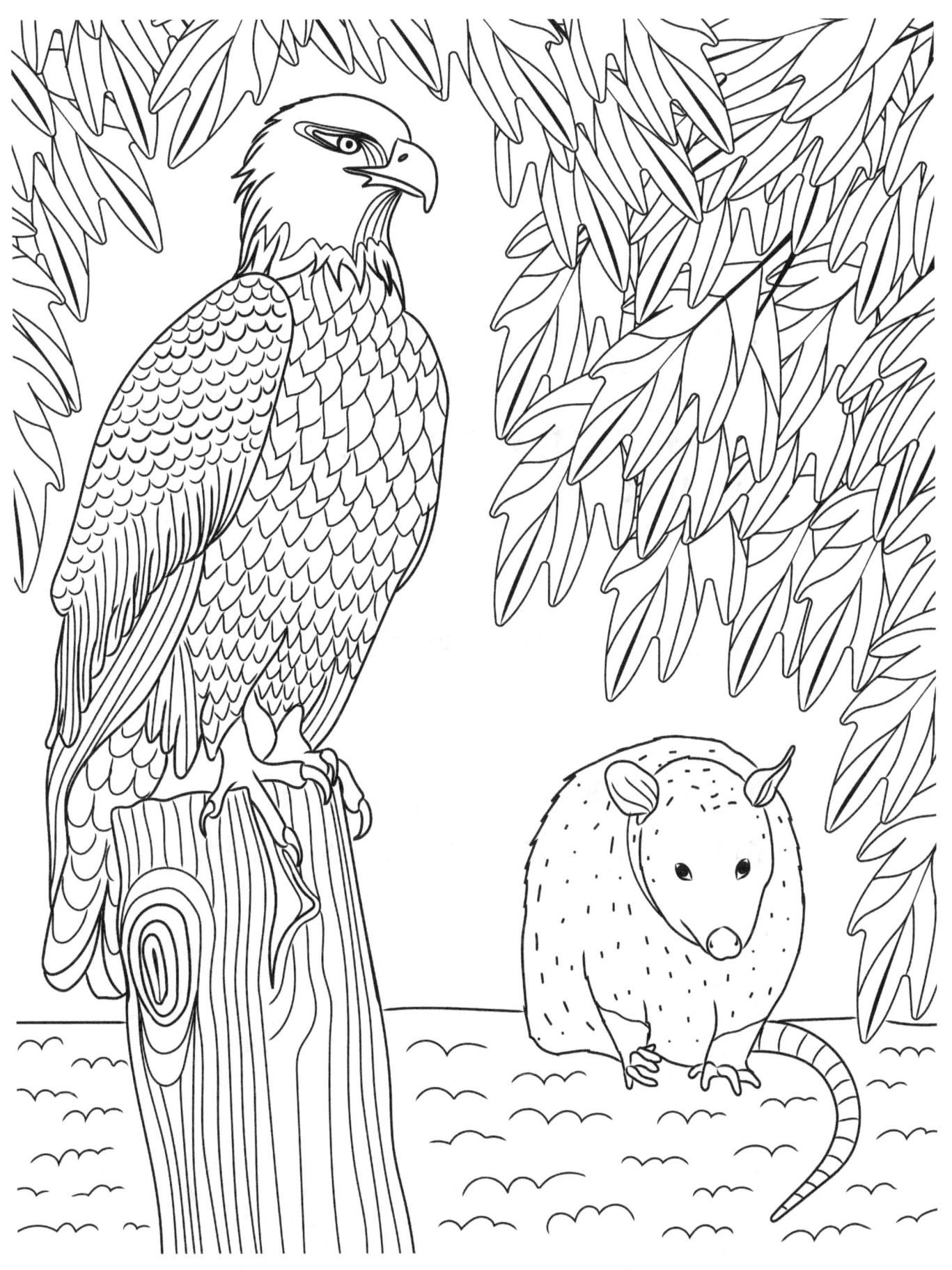

In the United States, President William Howard Taft created a Billy Possum to try and be as popular as the Teddy Bear.

Have you heard of this?

Yeah, we haven't either. The marketing effort didn't last a year.

The Billy Possum

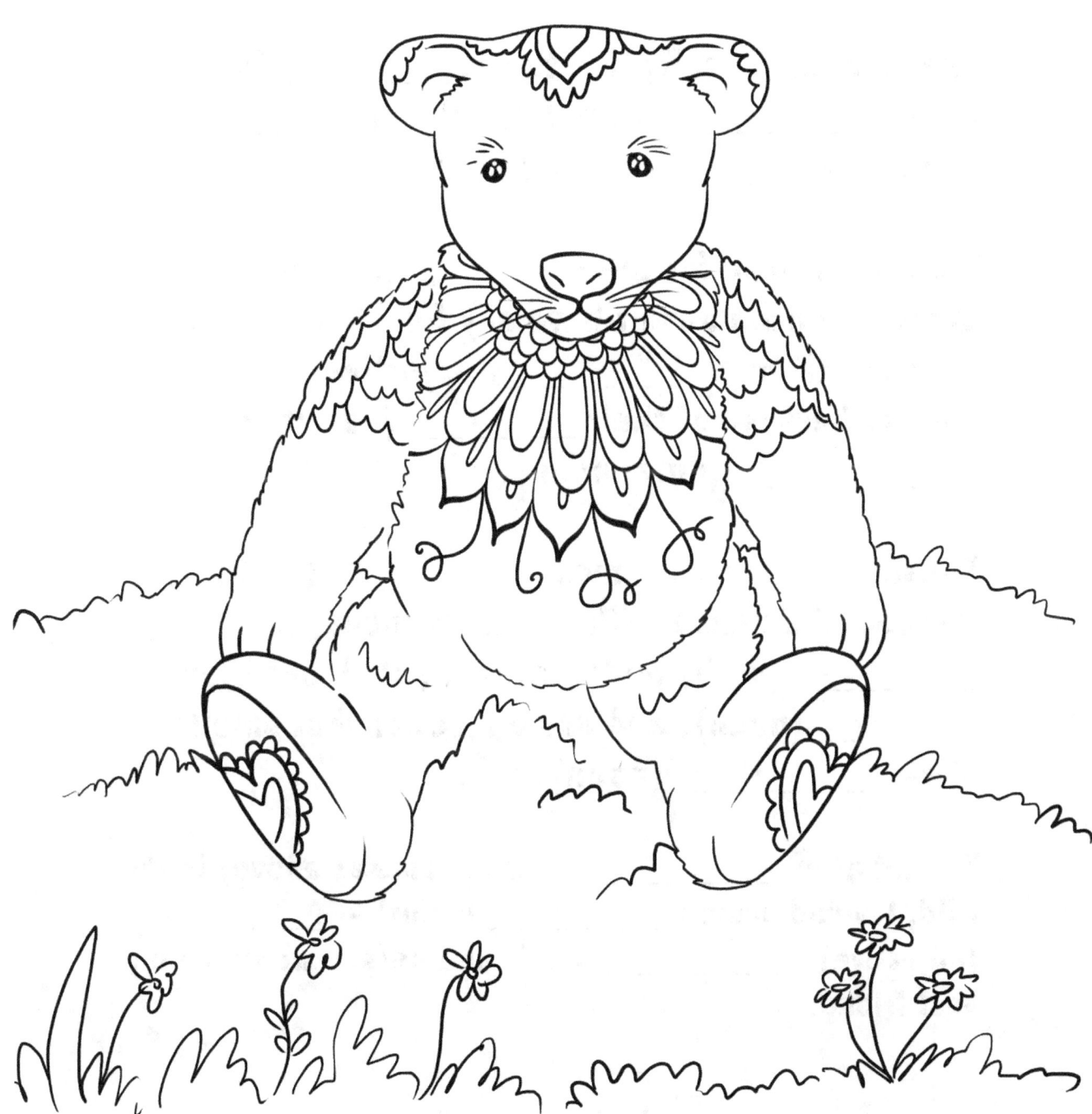

Time for an OPOSSUM-LIB!

The _____ (animal) is a scary looking but curiously cute animal found in most of _____ (place).

These animals really like to eat _____ (plural noun), _____ (plural noun), and _____ (adjective) _____ (plural noun).

They are known for their _____ (body part, plural), which doesn't have any fur. In fact, some describe them as _____ (adjective) _____ (noun) because of their _____ (adjective) _____ (plural noun).

These animals sometimes _____ (verb) as a method of defense. When this happens, they _____ (verb) on the ground, stick out their _____ (noun), and make an odor that smells like _____ (noun).

If I met a/an _____ (animal, same as above) in the wild, I would name it _____ (color) - _____ (adjective) _____ (noun), and he/she would be my best friend.

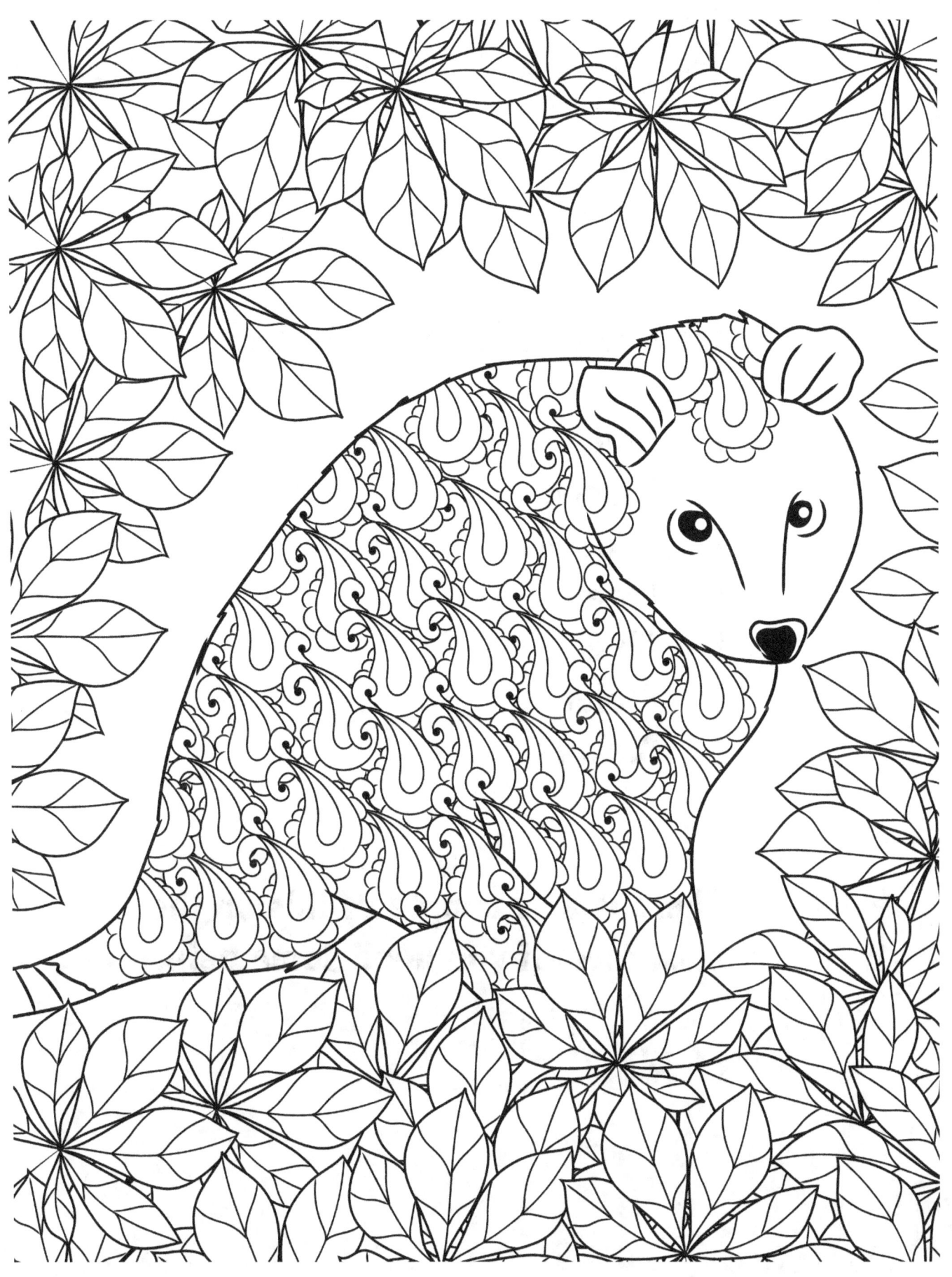

Let's color this one by letter!

A. Red
B. Orange
C. Yellow
D. Green
E. Blue
F. Violet
G. Brown

There is an example of this on the back cover if you need some help.

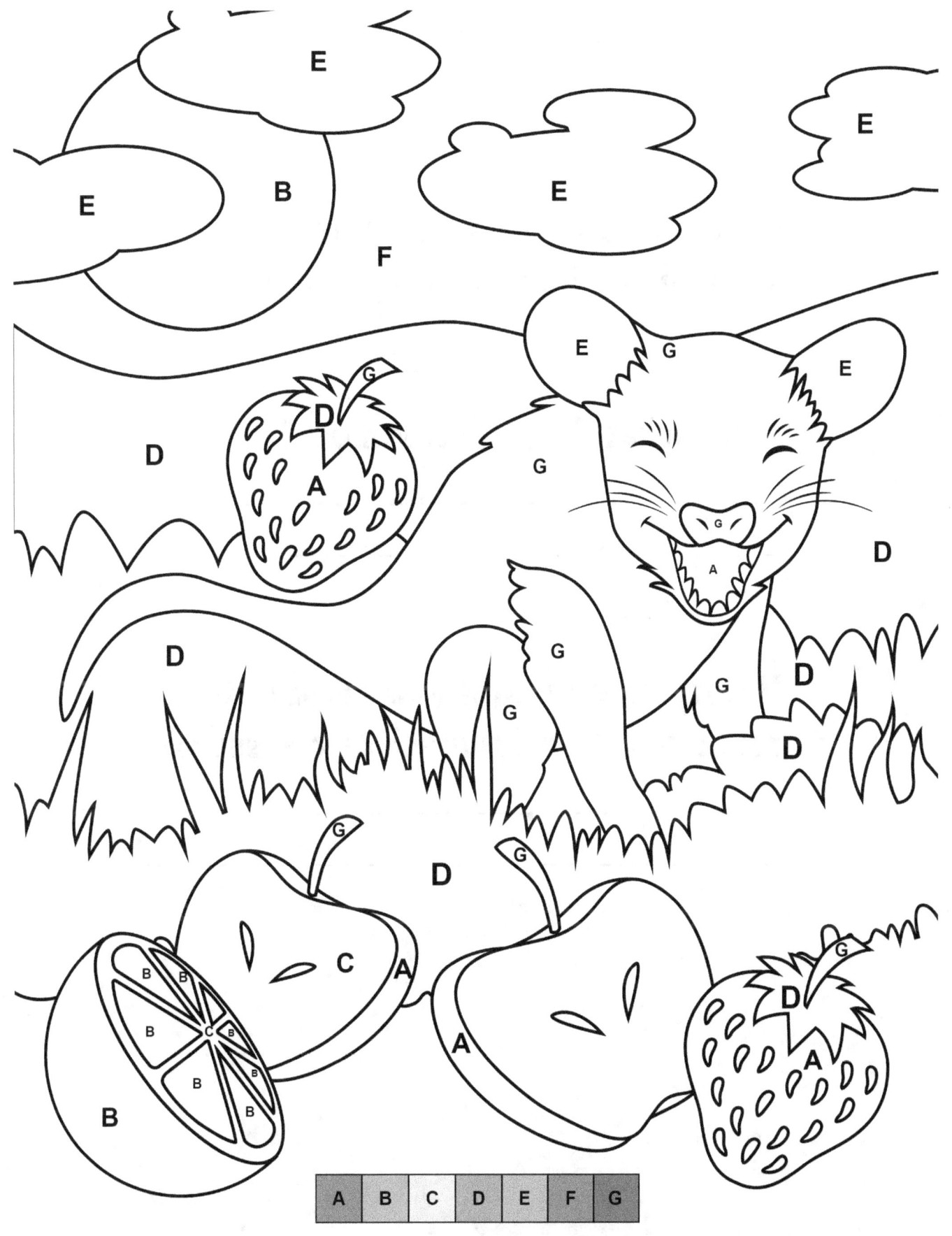

Have you ever seen an opossum (outside of this coloring book)?

If so, what do you remember?

_____

_____

If not, where might you be able to meet your first impossible opossum?

_____

_____

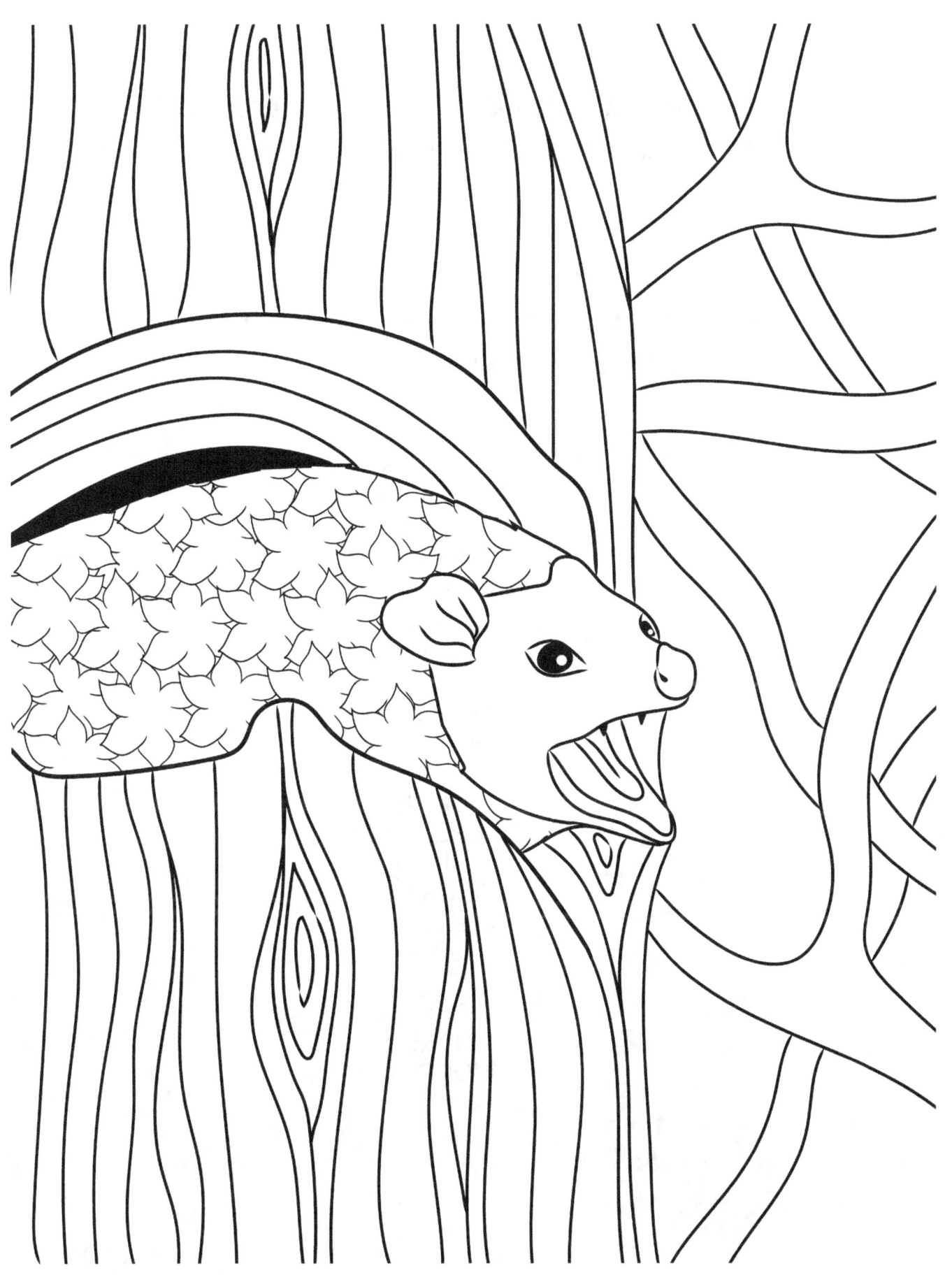

Wow, we've learned a lot about opossums in this book! That wasn't too impossible, was it?

See if you can find some of the things we've learned in this word search.

BANDICOOT
CAPYBARA
DEAD
FAINT
IMPOSSIBLY
JOEYS
MARSUPIAL
NEST
OPOSSUM
PANDA
PLAYING
POUCH
PREHENSILE
PUPILS
QUOKKA
RED
SNAKES
STINKY
TAIL
TICKS
WOMBAT

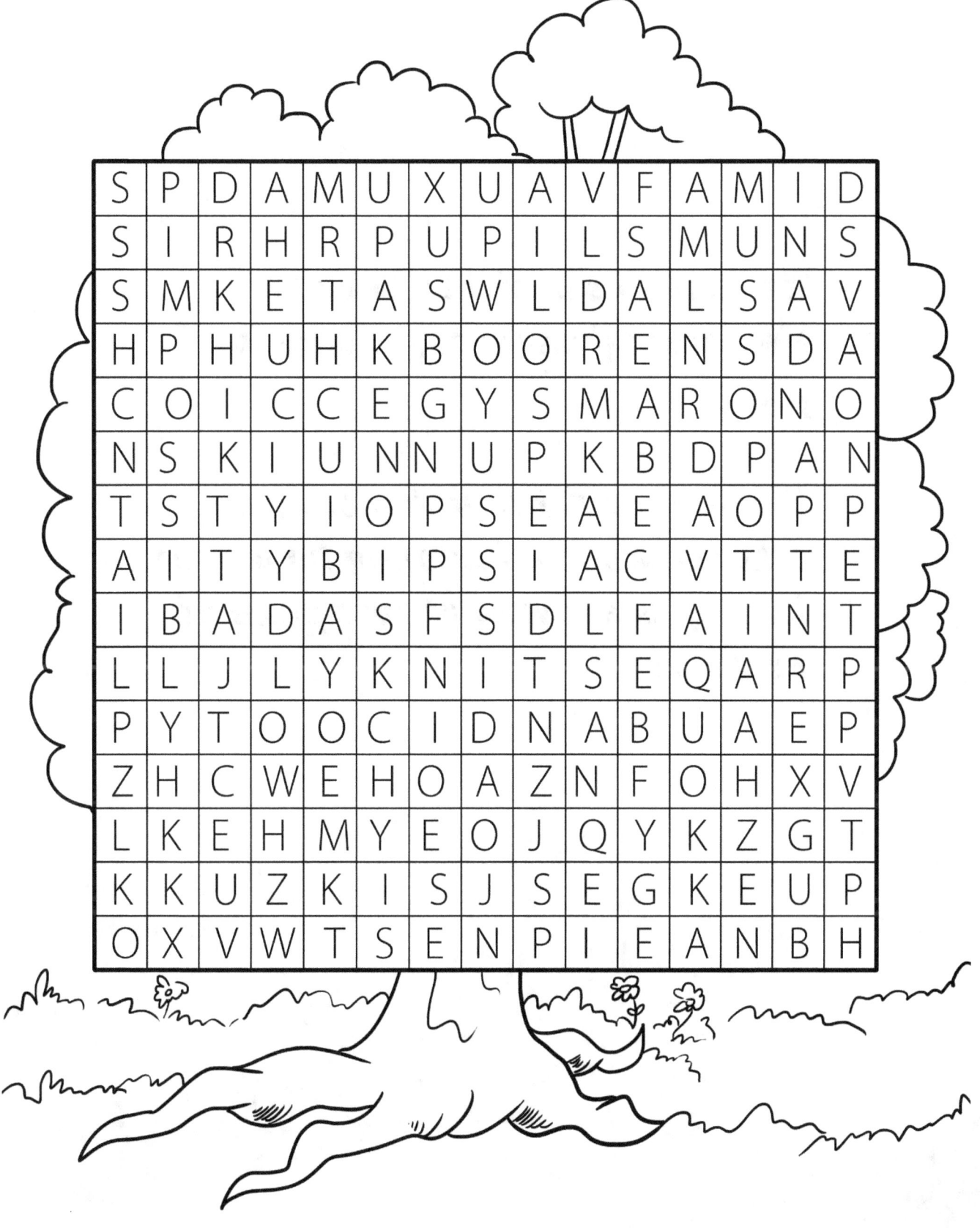

We hope this book has been an awesome opossum experience for you!

Please consider checking out our other educational coloring books and leaving us a review at your place of purchase.

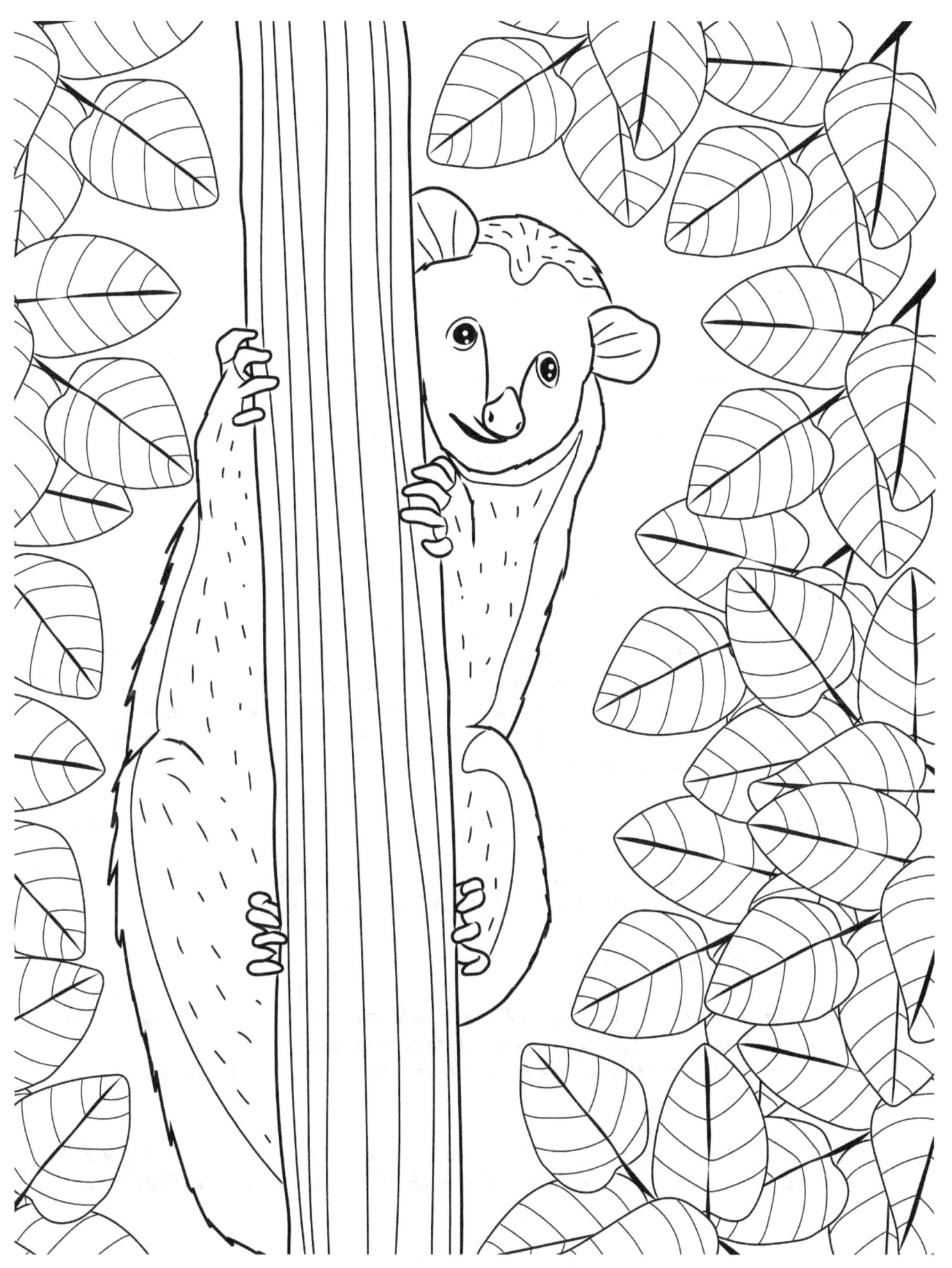

About the Editor

Jonathan Terry, DO, ABIHM, IFMCP is a board-certified osteopathic physician and surgeon, a general psychiatrist, a Diplomate of the American Board of Psychiatry and Neurology (ABPN), a Diplomate of the National Board of Physicians and Surgeons (NBPAS), and a Diplomate of the American Board of Integrative Holistic Medicine (ABIHM). He serves on faculty in several accredited medical schools, residency programs, and professional training programs. Dr. Terry is proud to be a National Health Service Corps Ambassador and works primarily with underserved populations, high-acuity inpatient psychiatric patients, and in consultation for program and policy-building initiatives. Dr. Terry's clinical interests include primary care consultation, nutrition, osteopathy, integrative medicine, kindness, and prevention.

Read more at www.DrJonathanTerry.com, and follow us on Facebook @MyCapybara and @DrJonathanTerry. Dr. Jonathan Terry is also on YouTube.

About the Book

Impossibly Opossum is about community investment and involvement at every level. International artists from underserved areas were independently interviewed and contracted as contributors to enthusiastically craft this unique, award-winning collection while providing investment in their local communities. Proceeds from the book are reinvested in local mental health initiatives including prevention, education, and providing free or discounted care to those without insurance, those who cannot access care, students, and impaired professionals.

We're especially proud to feature licensed artwork from *Desiree Albarran* from Bogotá, Colombia. Desiree likes to draw with all possible materials and techniques, making many funny characters that people love. She is a cat lover, cookie hunter, and assiduous gamer. See Desiree's portfolio at: https://www.behance.net/desireeart

Check Out Our Other Colorful Titles:

- *Eat The Rainbow* & the *Eat the Rainbow Coloring Book*
- *The Pursuit of Capyness: A Zen Capybara Coloring Book*
- *Red, White, and Panda: An Educational Red Panda Coloring Book for Adults and Children*

IF YOU LIKE THIS BOOK, PLEASE LEAVE US A REVIEW AT YOUR PURCHASE SITE! REVIEWS ARE SO IMPOSSUMABLY IMPORTANT FOR HELPING THIS BOOK HELP OTHER PEOPLE

www.ingramcontent.com/pod-product-compliance
Lightning Source LLC
Chambersburg PA
CBHW080505220526
45465CB00006B/2380